G000146431

# Escape from Purgatory

## by

## Joseph R. Schofield, Jr.

### First edition

### Published by:
### Matthew 10:32 Ministries, ltd. co.

**A Personal Note from the Author**

Dear friend: Writing this book has allowed me to touch many lives for Christ. At the start of his Gospel, Luke describes his efforts to carefully investigate everything he has written. I too, have tried to carefully analyze my subject matter; in this case, the teachings of Roman Catholicism in light of Scripture. Having been a Catholic for over 35 years necessitated a diligent, cautious, and repetitious study of the topics in this book Whether you agree or disagree with my conclusions, may God bless your time exploring His truths.

# Escape from Purgatory

## by Joseph R. Schofield, Jr.

**Published by:**

Matthew 10:32 Ministries, ltd. co.

Post Office Box 20547

Albuquerque, N. M. 87154

**Library of Congress Catalog Card Number:   93-80481**

Schofield, Joseph R., Jr.

Escape From Purgatory / by Joseph R. Schofield, Jr.

Includes index.

ISBN: 0-9639271-1-6   $11.95 Softcover

*This book is dedicated to*

*the rider on the white horse*

*in Revelation 19:11.*

# Acknowledgments

Unless otherwise noted, all Scripture references throughout this document are cited from the NIV Study Bible, Copyright 1985 by the Zondervan Corporation. The following acknowledgment has been requested by the publisher to appear on the title page of works that reference the NIV. "Scripture taken from the HOLY BIBLE, NEW INTERNATIONAL VERSION. Copyright 1973, 1978, 1984 International Bible Society. Used by permission of Zondervan Bible Publishers."

I gratefully acknowledge the use of Dr. D. Russell Humphreys ideas in understanding and relaying the scientific evidence for a much younger earth then many of us may have learned. His article, "Evidence for a Young Universe," is referenced in the first chapter.

I gratefully acknowledge the work of Grant Jeffrey who has provided motivation and scholarship regarding the nation of Israel and end times prophecy. His book Armageddon Appointment with Destiny, is also mentioned in Chapter 1.

# Table of Contents

# A Synoptic Table of Contents

## Introduction

This book is written to glorify God, to establish or improve our relationship with Him. Our time is expiring and yet God's timing is perfect in all things committed unto Him. We know God by many names; yet, He is one God.

A Kinder and Gentler Message (This Isn't It): We need some straight truth in a world of chaos. Different models exist for understanding our relationship with God. God and His Word are inseparable.

How Can We Relate to the Bible Given Our Worldly Knowledge Today?: We can use the Word of God to enhance our understanding of the knowledge of the world. We can use the knowledge of the world to improve our understanding of the Bible. We can use both of these precepts interchangeably; but typically, one of them dominates how we accumulate and accept knowledge.

## Chapter 1

The Bible–A Credible An Incredible Source: The Bible is a most credible source of knowledge and wisdom. Matthew explains many fulfilled prophecies.

Prophecy From the Very First Book: The prophetic nature of God's Word begins with the first book of the Bible and continues to the very last. The "minor" prophets played major roles in revealing God's promises. Because of the Scripture we knew Christ was coming and we know He's coming again.

Some Prophecies Concerning the Nation of Israel: The prophecies of the Bible center on the nation of Israel–His firstborn. Daniel and Ezekiel offer amazingly accurate prophesies of events that have been fulfilled and others awaiting fulfillment.

Brief Archaeological Evidence and Scripture: The miracles in the Bible are from God. Science has attempted to explain those miracles with unscientific assertions. With growing regularity, both from historical and archaeological perspectives, the Bible is proven accurate and correct.

When Science Meets Scripture: Scientists prove that science is not the right answer. Ministries exist solely for demonstrating the accuracy of God's Word over man's hypotheses.

The Bible–Taking It Personally: I did. I still do. The Bible changed my life and it altered my desire to grow through the Word. We need to know God's Word and then "take it personally" and put it to use in our own lives.

## Chapter 2

Tradition: Its Origins and the Catholic Church: Tradition is a cornerstone of Catholicism. The Bible teaches us about traditions especially in light of the Word. Tradition is reviewed from a Biblical viewpoint.

The Returning Christ–No Babe in a Manger: The purpose of Christ's second coming is not the same as His first. Jesus taught and exemplified love and yet He also rebuked and warned. When the Son of God comes again in the clouds He will not be the babe in a manger..

The Value of Fear: The Bible repeatedly tells us not to fear things other than God. Throughout the Bible we are told to fear (revere) God. Fear has positively impacted the Church.

What's Wrong With This Picture? Tradition and culture are breaking God's commands. God's Word is diffused by stained glass windows when we use the windows to shut God out rather than to let His Word shine through.

Historically, the Catholic Church Has Taught That it is the Only Church: Various popes and councils declare their sovereignty and indoctrinate through the Catholic church.

## Chapter 3

Peter Principle or Principal? The origin of the word "pope" defies God's directive. The head of the Church and the head of man is God himself. Jesus did not establish the office of the pope.

A Simple Model For Scriptural Interpretation: Models of this world that help us understand God's Word can be useful. These models may occur in different fields of study. The discipline of software engineering and its approaches to software testing can be a start for testing our understanding of Scripture.

Peter–Legacy, Residency, or Supremacy? Peter could not have been the first pope. Peter may never have been a resident of Rome. Peter did not claim to be a pope, nor did he treat anyone like many of the popes throughout history.

Well Then, What About the Other Popes? The popes have perpetrated some of the most heinous acts in global history. These acts are documented in a number of texts but receive little attention today when Rome asserts a lineage from Peter for its authority. Murder, rape, incest, and devil worship do little to support the notion of the pope as the Vicar of Christ image.

A Brief Examination of Indulgences and Purgatory: The motive behind purgatory was greed, not cleansing. The Catholic church adds to the books of the Bible to substantiate even a remote misinterpretation of the concept of purgatory. Purgatory is a fictional place where man makes the atonement for his sins disregarding God's plan.

Why Escape from Purgatory? The title suggests being held against one's will. The Catholic church, the self-proclaimed only true church outside of which there is no salvation, is characteristically cultic. Its members are often held by tactics of guilt and fear (of the church and its doctrines not God).

Celibacy–God's Plan or Man's? Celibacy was not practiced by Peter, nor required by Jesus, nor part of early church doctrine. The practice of celibacy paved the way for further acts of indiscretion throughout the Catholic church hierarchy. Celibacy is still another of man's plans to establish his own righteousness.

But the More Recent Popes Are Better–Right? The popes continue to rule of the traditions of their predecessors. Bowing, kissing, and other acts in reverence and respect were not allowed by Peter and Biblical teaching. Papal infallibility and irreversibility positions the pope as a "god" in his own right (or his own sight).

**Chapter 4**

Mary–What Have They Done to You? Mary was the virgin mother of Jesus. Mary has been venerated well beyond Scripture. The sinless nature of Mary contradicts Scripture. Prayers to Mary that call upon her intercessory power contradict her own words. The Ascension of Mary is not found in the Bible. The Catholic church needed 1900 years to accept this doctrine.

<u>Mary as Intercessor</u>: The Biblical account of Saul and Samuel in First Samuel 28 depicts a very different outcome for those who contact the dead to intercede. Jesus taught that He alone was the way, truth, and life. The need for a "mother god" is not new and its pagan origins precede Christianity.

<u>Mary's Perpetual Virginity</u>: Jesus had brothers and sisters. Joseph withheld normal relations with his wife until after Jesus was born (Matthew 1:25).

<u>Veneration of Mary</u>: The church has devised many techniques for turning our attention away from Christ. The Marian year, rosaries, statues, special sacrifices (of the mass), devotions, and prayers, are a few examples. Jesus did not pray to His mother. Jesus prayed only to the Father. Salvation is obtained through Christ only.

<u>The Holy Run Around</u>: Praying to Mary, invoking her name, and trusting in any entity other than God is not in accordance with His plan. Our needs are met by Him directly.

<u>Reported Appearances of Mary</u>: Catholic church history is rich with reported appearances of Mary. John taught us how to test the Spirits in his first epistle. The use of secrets to inveigle witnesses to Christ is not a Biblical approach. Words used to glorify an image misdirect the glory. Recent observances in Yugoslavia are not endorsed by the Catholic church and have occult overtones.

<u>Mary—A Redefined Role Under Second Vatican Council</u>: Mary is now the "new Eve." Praying to Mary and to God are deemed acceptable since they are on "different levels." The removal of Marian statues, rosaries, scapulars, and other idolatrous objects has not occurred "universally" throughout the universal church.

**Chapter 5**

<u>Selected Doctrines on the Sacraments of Roman Catholicism</u>: The sacraments, as instruments of salvation, are alive and well in the Catholic church. Justification by works thrives. The commandments of the church are of equal salvational importance as the commandments of God. The parole system of purgatory continues.

<u>Selected Doctrines Surrounding the Sacraments</u>: Seven is the proper number of sacraments although still unconfirmed by Scripture. The only administrator of the sacraments is the Catholic church.

Selected Doctrines on the Sacrament of Baptism:  Catholic baptism continues to be necessary for salvation.  Jesus was baptized at 30 and as a witness, not for salvation.  Catholicism continues to teach that "sponsorship" (godparents) can speak on behalf of an infant and in effect to make their "acceptance" decision in their behalf.

Selected Doctrine On the Sacrament of Confirmation:  The Catholic church teaches that through confirmation, the participant receives the Holy Spirit.  Yet, the gift of the Spirit comes from God per His timing and not traditions and ceremonies.

Selected Doctrines On the Sacrament of Confession:  Jesus taught us to take our sins to the Father in the Lord's Prayer.  John taught us to confess so that our sins would be forgiven.  Neither taught penance.  Neither taught confession to a priest, which, ironically parallels the Old Testament law and the Old Covenant.  Only God can forgive man's sins.  We can forgive one another but we still need His forgiveness, for whenever we sin, we sin against God.  Paul taught us to be reconciled to God.

**Chapter 6**

Selected Doctrines On the Mass:  Still the "sacrifice of the mass", this daily occurrence uses the blood of Christ to atone for recent sins and the sins of the dead.  This offering is contrary to Christ's proclamation from the cross that "it is finished."  Any sacrifice to imitate Christ's dishonors the price He's already paid.

Masses in Honor of the "Saints":  Jesus never prayed to or for the dead.  He did not assemble the crowds in honor of Old Testament "saints."  The effectiveness of prayer in Luke 16 to a dead person was unsuccessful.  Masses in honor of the departed are driven, in part, by the possibility of their residency in purgatory (according to Catholic tradition).  The popes continue to ask saints to intercede for us.

Only the Catholic Church Understands Things of a Divine Nature:  Over 1000 uses of the word "know" in the Word ensure us of our confidence in Christ as His children.  Catholic tradition teaches that it alone has authority for defining the teachings and interpretations of the Bible.

**Chapter 7**

The Good News from Second Vatican Council (Sounds a Lot Like the Bad News from Earlier Councils):  Attempts through Second Vatican

Council attempts to give a different appearance to Catholicism, seemed to have worked; but, every underlying doctrine of Catholic teaching remains unchanged. Earlier councils and teachings are endorsed by the papacy during Second Vatican Council.

The Crusades Continue (In Verbal Form): The tone and teachings of the Catholic church for all non-Catholics are uncomplimentary. The Second Vatican Council is criticized by varying interest groups within the Catholic church. Protestants are still considered "separated brethren" while Rome does little to address Christian movements. The traditions of the Catholic church march onward in the day-to-day life of Catholics and any hope of movement towards Scriptural integrity is averted.

**Chapter 8**

The Best of the Rest: The best is yet to come. Christians are called to be prepared and active witnesses for God's coming kingdom. This final chapter offers motivation and opportunities for improving our relationship with Christ.

Jesus Is Returning (and He Is Returning Soon!): The signs of Christ's return are converging all around us. The world is in unprecedented turmoil. Our own country is bankrupt. Most importantly, the nation of Israel is making its own preparations for the return of Christ. The rise of the Antichrist and the revived Roman empire are promised and signs of their appearing are evident. Christ's return has been prophesied since He returned to the Father. It grows closer every day.

Selling Life Insurance versus Sharing Life Assurance: To sell insurance requires a buyer and a seller. To share life assurance requires a giver and a receiver; no exchange of money occurs and the giver is blessed just like the receiver. We are all called to share. We are all called first.

What's It To You? God got my attention. God faithfully protected me even when I did not walk with Him. All along the Lord sent other Christians in my direction. God gives an outline of the equipment He has provided us. Put it on and be prepared to serve.

Who Do You Say That I Am? Scripture answers this question adequately. Christ himself gave us the answer. Those who knew Him proclaimed His identity. A summary of who He is in every book of the Bible is portrayed. This is the God we are called to know personally.

<u>The Last Exodus</u>:  God intervened to rescue His children in mass from Egypt about 3500 years ago.  We too need to call upon the Lord to hear our afflictions.  He has promised to "Exodus" His believers out of this world.  Be encouraged and look forward to His coming.

<u>Could You Be Convicted (of Being a Christian)</u>?  We need to put our witnessing to work.  The home, car, and workplace are all places were we could put our faith to work while being simultaneously tested.  Evidence of our faith can be found in what we watch, do, read, wear, say, and think.  Ultimately, Christ is the judge and the verdict has already been handed to the jury for believers.

# Disclaimer

After over 20 years of ministering the Word, the apostle Paul offered the following observation:

"Not that I have already obtained all this, or have already been made perfect, but I press on to take hold of that for which Christ Jesus took hold of me." (Philippians 3:12)

This passage from Paul underscores the importance of recognizing the imperfect state of man in general and the author in particular. This author does not pretend to be complete in his scholarship of the following materials nor correct on every opinion offered regarding God's Word. I do not pretend to be a prophet with some new insight or teaching thereby encouraging a new following or sect, nor do I seek glory for myself. The writer in Hebrews describes this feeling.

"In the past God spoke to our forefathers through the prophets at many times and in various ways, but in these last days he has spoken to us by his Son, whom he appointed heir of all things, and through whom he made the universe." (Hebrews 1:1 - 2)

In this context, the Son has the answers; I offer but one possible interpretation based on personal research and experience.

This book potentially includes typographical errors and unintended errors in interpretation. The final and only true authority in the matters of God is God Himself. Neither the author, nor the publisher, nor the printer shall be liable or responsible to any entity, legal or otherwise, or person or persons, regarding any loss or damage, or alleged loss or damage due directly or indirectly to the information and ideas expressed or implied in this book. Your continued reading, in part or in full, of this material serves as your acceptance of this admittance.

The thoughts in this book are mine (and perhaps others), not the thoughts of God. Isaiah reminds each of us

"For my thoughts are not your thoughts, neither are your ways my ways' declares the Lord.  'As the heavens are higher than the earth, so are my ways higher than your ways and my thoughts than your thoughts." (Isaiah 55:8 - 9)

As Paul wrote to the Philippians he also concluded that he "pressed on" to do the work for which he was called to do.  Paul's call was to obedience.  My prayer is nothing less.

*This is not the tale of my life,*

*but the story of true life!*

# Escape from Purgatory

## Introduction

Our primary purpose as Christians is to know and glorify God. This purpose, seeking His will, His purpose, and His plan, is both evident and consistent throughout Scripture. We know that we, as was all creation, were formed for His pleasure and it pleases Him when we seek His presence and His will.

How specifically might this book serve to glorify God? First, in accordance with Matthew 28:18-20, we are all commissioned to spread His word and His plan for our salvation. Christ's message is a message of love for His creation. Care will be taken to direct Scriptural references towards Catholicism not Catholics; towards the institution and not its constituents. According to Ephesians 6:12 the enemy has entangled us in a spiritual war and the enemy is not the Catholic but rather the evil one who has been sinning from the beginning. For this reason I have made a deliberate attempt to avoid the use of emotion-filled words like aberrant, anathema, heretical, and polemic unless quoting the doctrines of the Catholic church in which case the use of such language is unavoidable.

We glorify God when we obey Him with joyful and spirit-filled hearts.

"Whatever you do, work at it with all your heart, as working for the Lord, not for men." (Colossians 3:23)

Second, we glorify our Lord when we dwell on His Scripture and share our faith with others. My thoughts are based on the Bible plus personal experiences through which I believe Christ worked in my life. I pray that the words I select glorify Him and that those words also serve to establish or improve your personal relationship with the savior.

An improved personal relationship with the Father through Jesus is a third purpose for this book. This relationship, the source of our salvation, is a free gift of grace from God. This free gift is offered to everyone and is made available through His atonement on the cross. No good works, no ceremonies, and no substitutes are provided within God's

Holy Word–penned by men yet worded by God.  These same writings have been accepted as authentic throughout the past two millennia and accepted at the very foundations of the church while still others were meticulously and scrupulously reviewed and rejected.

A fourth purpose this material may serve is to help those who witness to the Catholic community understand some essential differences between Catholicism and Christianity.  Where Catholicism leaves the confines of Scripture, it does not add tradition to Scripture but contradicts it. Christians are called to be prepared to give an account for the hope they have in 1 Peter 3:15.

> "  ... Always be prepared to give an answer to everyone who asks you to give the reason for the hope that you have. ..."

The numerous examples illustrated throughout this book, leave little room for denying that tradition has supplanted Scripture in both practice and doctrine, in importance in the Catholic church .

Other motives provide an incentive for researching and presenting this book.  One motive would be to reach the number of family members and friends with whom I do not take the time to witness.  I have seen friends dying to whom I had no witness, yet knew that they were under Catholicism.  Not that this precluded their salvation, but rather that I know there are enough distractions from the truth to have rendered salvation difficult under the best of circumstances.

Obviously my personal testimony and experiences are restricted to those I encounter on a day-to-day basis.  I pray this book will provide a vehicle to reach others.  I do not have a worldwide television ministry or even a local radio program.  But I do have a truth-based message of faith, hope, and love that will be available through this book.  This message can now reach those who are not sure why they belong to a certain church and those who know there must be something in closer adherence to Scripture on which to cling.

Another motivation for writing this book is the urgency I feel for the imminent return of Christ Himself.  I spend more time on this subject in the final chapter.  My recent research of historical and contemporary prophecy scholars all seem to indicate the time for salvation is short and this offer of salvation will not always be with us.

Through this book I give thanks to a number of people who have been a special influence along the way.  Many of them would not have recognized their influence when the seed was first planted. It would have seemed to them as the seed that fell on the stony path; temporary and easily swept away. But let me reassure you what may have appeared at best to have been the stony path has become a mighty foundation stone, the petra in my life.

One such influence was Mary; a former work associate I was able to contact in February of 1992. She had spent a couple of years hearing me ask difficult questions about the Bible and Jesus. Actually, she describes me then as "just a young punk." After twelve years of no contact, I was able to share with Mary that I had resolved the very questions with which I challenged her. Through conversation, Mary came to hear that my joy germinated and grew so much fuller, and that I had to share the manifestation of my joy with her. I hope the few minutes we spent on the phone that night blessed her as her faith once blessed me.

I am uniquely unqualified to author a book. I am not a pastor, nor a church official. I am not the president of a company or on the board of directors of any multinational conglomerate. I am not a seminary student and do not possess a Ph.D. I do not know Greek or Hebrew. I am not a perfect husband, father, son, worker, servant, or neighbor. I am a sinner. I have made tremendous mistakes and horrible decisions; have been and may still be, at times, a most unworthy witness for Christ and His bride the church.

Yet, I possess a burning greed to know God and to know about Him. I can attest to personal rescues, healings, and specific answered prayers. I know there is something other than my worldliness that provided my comfort during and through difficult times. I have earnestly prayed God would confiscate the time and resources necessary to write this book if its writing was not in accordance with His perfect will and purpose. I also recognize my obligation to practice self-control with the talents and interests with which He has blessed me. I think the apostle Paul, after 30 years of Christian walk, said it best in Philippians:

> "Not that I have already obtained all this, or have already been made perfect, but I press on to take hold of that for which Christ Jesus took hold of me. Brothers, I do not consider myself yet to have taken hold of it. But one thing I do: Forgetting what is behind and straining toward what is ahead," (Philippians 3:12 - 13)

My prevailing dilemma is how to start with this material. Please be patient as I share the following difficulty. I struggled with various possible approaches to this book. One approach is to deliver a clear strong message of repentance and salvation early and to ensure the message was delivered in the event the reader did not make it to the second page. I want to deliver a message based in Scripture which seems to necessitate an apologetic approach first defending Scripture, believing that my 38 years under Catholicism provides me with a real opportunity to move from the experiential to the Scriptural. Still another technique would involve an autobiographical approach to my own walk; yet, this is not the tale of my life, but the story of true life!!!

My synonymous use of the words God, Jesus, Christ, Creator, Intercessor, Mediator, Jehovah, Redeemer, Immanuel, Lord, Living Word, Word of God, King of Kings, Lord of Lords, Lamb of God, Father, Savior, etc., I believe all describe the God of the old and new testaments. Apart from Him there is no other God. The concept of the Trinity also confirms God is but a single entity viewed by us as unique yet inseparable persons. I was also raised (or trained) to capitalize pronouns that referred to God. As I continue through the development of this text I can hardly understand why I might capitalize "I", (other than to follow the rules of the English language) yet treat any reference to God as somehow less "proper." Holy, holy, is His name. I will exalt His name forever.

## A Kinder and Gentler Message (This Isn't It)

This is a new age, an age with an emerging new world order, an age of kinder and gentler messages, an age in which man continues to exalt the created instead of the creator, where abortion soars, where drugs ruin, where chaos characterizes the business world, where prayer takes a seat outside the classroom while promiscuity moves to the front of the class, an age of decaying family and moral values, where the stadiums fill and the sanctuaries empty, an age desperately in need of some straight truth. Ministries avoid direct mention of other denomination or religion. Instead those ministries concentrate on winning souls to Christ by offering the good news of Jesus Christ. The world continues to need these ministries.

Few ministries are willing to reach those entrenched in non-scriptural beliefs. The few that do, tend to be either threatened at times or depicted as less than Christian at other times. My message will attempt to articulate the vast differences between Catholic tradition and Scripture. My intent is to provide information in an age where information is increasingly available through technology. The "kinder and gentler" messages of the past have not reached over 50 million Catholics in the United States alone, and 18 times that number worldwide. The "kinder and gentler" messages have failed to penetrate the hearts of folks who are deeply indoctrinated in a system and void of a personal relationship with the almighty God. This message can serve to uproot those entrenched in a belief system significantly different from the one Christ left with us.

Another pervasive attitude is reflected in the avoidance of our discussion of the Scriptures because of its sometimes controversial subject matter. In essence, this caution is often rooted in not knowing what the Scripture says and is manifested in an unwillingness and a discomfort to witness or testify on its behalf. Avoiding discussion of the Bible because of the diversity of opinions about what it means is not Scriptural either. We are implored to search for the truth using Scripture as the basis and to share it in love.

## How Can We Relate to the Bible Given Our Worldly Knowledge Today?

A prayer partner of mine, who is a seminary graduate, describes a two-variant model for understanding our growth with God. The first variant suggests that we use our knowledge (worldly) to develop our faith. This variation might for instance draw on archaeological evidence of Christ's life, the early church, the nation of Israel, and the temple as sufficient justification for belief in the existence of God. By further evidencing Jesus' miracles, His death, and the events surrounding His tomb (even as recorded by non-believing historians during Christ's time on earth), one could accept that Jesus was whom He claimed to be. From this evidence, one could be motivated to accept Christ and build a faith from additional research and experience.

The second variant is exactly the opposite; that we use our faith to shape our knowledge. This variation suggests that without any question, some may accept Christ prior to obtaining vast worldly knowledge. Perhaps this acceptance is based on family devotions, Christian parents, miracles, or other Godly influences in the believer's life. All other worldly knowledge now becomes subject to this "faith first" filter.

Characteristically, this believer is likely to question science and history as quickly as non-believers doubt the authenticity of the Bible.

Other variants arise as combinations of the world-based-faith and faith-based-world variants are experienced in phases of the believer's life. For instance, I tend to believe that Hal Lindsey's writings, and subsequent examination with Scripture molded me in the early 70s into a world-based-faith. Since the early 80s I have been driven by a faith-based-world taking everything into account through the Scriptures. How reassured I feel when I hear that history books are being rewritten as archaeology unfolds and the original Biblical writings are found to be absolutely precise in every detail.

It might be worth examining our own disposition to this model and its ramifications. Not that either is preferred, but that both can help explain our own journeys and life changing moments. Where are you in this context? Where have you been? Where are you headed? What events may have changed your own framework for sorting and accepting the acts of faith and the acts of knowledge?

In an attempt to establish a foundation for Biblical belief and accuracy we cannot ignore the Bible, if we do we ignore one of the greatest gifts God bestowed upon us. The greatest gift of course must be Christ's sacrifice for us. Another great gift is the Holy Spirit, the Paraclete, the great comforter who was sent to us to complete our needed knowledge and relationship with the Father. John describes why the Bible is such a great gift.

> "In the beginning was the Word, and the Word was with God, and the Word was God. He was with God in the beginning." (John 1:1)

John continues in opening another Book.

> "That which was from beginning, which we have heard, which we have seen with our eyes, which we have looked at and our hands have touched–this we proclaim concerning the Word of life." (1 John 1:1)

According to the Apostle John's writings and the Spirit's leading the Word was God. That same Word, the essence of God, is with us today; it hasn't changed and it is not yet fulfilled in its entirety. The best, the returning Christ, is yet to come. Stay tuned, or in a more excellent way–believe, as the mystery of Corinthians 15 unfolds.

"Listen, I tell you a mystery:  We will not all sleep, but we will all be changed—in a flash, in the twinkling of an eye, at the last trumpet.  For the trumpet will sound, the dead will be raised imperishable, and we will be changed."
(1 Corinthians 15:51)

Until that trumpet sounds, we rest assured of knowing the truths of the God's Word.  Therefore, the following Biblical truths help to lay a foundation set not upon sand.

*I don't want Him to accept me*

*in accordance with my plan,*

*I want to ensure that I receive Him*

*in accordance with His plan!*

# Chapter 1

## The Bible A Credible An Incredible Source

We've all heard the familiar cliché "do it by the book." It seemed to have been drilled into me during my years of military service. The phrase continues to be used in conjunction with jobs that include very little flexibility and even less thought. Now when I apply the phrase it is after deliberate premeditation.

This chapter is not devoted to convincing anyone about the absolute accuracy of the Bible. Others have provided numerous texts that irrefutably contend beyond any reasonable doubt the Bible's validity. Instead, let us consider a few truths so either a curiosity for or an affirmation of the Scriptures may develop.

Sometimes we do a disservice to the Word of God when we use the testimony of high profile public figures as if we can grasp their words more easily than the Word. We can however, use the testimony of public figures concerning the value of the Bible. Abraham Lincoln described the Bible as the best gift God has given to man and the source of knowing right from wrong. Not that any man's words should be weighed more heavily than the testimony of the writers of Scripture but rather such words demonstrate the glory of God as inherited from generation to generation.

My love for Scripture evolved from the testimony and evidence of prophecy. Prophecy can be divided into two types: fulfilled and unfulfilled. At times disagreement arises as to whether a prophecy has been fulfilled, or not, by the occurrence of a particular event.   An example of such disagreement occurred in early 1991 as part of the conflict with Iraq.  The book of Jeremiah contains references to "smart arrows and weapons."  Some Christians have interpreted the cruise missile as the weapon that fulfilled this prophecy.  Other Christians are not as sure.  Then, a year after the war ended we learned our weapons did not destroy as many missile launchers as had earlier been believed.  We discovered that civilian targets were accidentally hit.   We recognized early in the war that our "smart weapons" could not distinguish between friendly and hostile forces.  I believe when God sets forth "the smart weapons" they will be far smarter than those we have mastered today.

While many prophecies may be adjacent in Scripture, we cannot assume they are fulfilled together.   Examples of partially fulfilled prophecy can be found in the book of Daniel Chapters 9 and 11.

Let's examine fulfilled prophecies, as described by Matthew in the first book of the New Testament.  Matthew's gospel has been called the most "read" book in all the Bible.  Part of this reasoning stems from new Bible readers avoiding the length or relevancy of the Old Testament.  Another reason is that some new Bible readers want to concentrate on the life of Jesus.  Still others are warned to stay away from books like Revelation because the imagery may be overwhelming.

- Very early in Matthew's account, even in his first chapter, as Joseph contemplates his relationship with the pregnant Mary, he is visited by an angel who offers him reassurance and reminds him that

  "All this took place to fulfill what the Lord had said through the prophet."  (Matthew 1:22)

- Later the disturbed Herod heard from the Magi that the King of the Jews had been born, and after he had asked his own counsel where Christ was to be born he was told

  "... In Bethlehem in Judea" they replied, "for this is what the prophet has written ..."  (Matthew 2:5)

- Matthew 2 reveals another fulfilled prophecy after the enraged Herod realized he had been tricked and ordered the killing of the boys two years old and younger

"Then what was said through the prophet Jeremiah was fulfilled" (Matthew 2:17)

- When Joseph, Mary, and Joseph returned to Israel after having lived in Egypt after their escape from Herod, we find

"and he went and lived in a town called Nazareth. So was fulfilled what was said through the prophets: 'He will be called a Nazarene'." (Matthew 2:23)

- When Jesus began His own ministry just after hearing John the Baptist had been jailed, he went to live in Capernaum "to fulfill what was said through the prophet Isaiah:".

- Jesus provides us with His purpose.

"Do not think that I have come to abolish the Law or the Prophets; I have not come to abolish them but to fulfill them." (Matthew 5:17)

- Jesus' tells us how that purpose would lead to a healing ministry.

"This was to fulfill what was spoken through the prophet Isaiah: 'He took up our infirmities and carried our diseases'." (Matthew 8:17)

- Upon healing many afflicted believers, Jesus warned the healed not to tell anyone who He was so as to not draw too much attention to His healing rather than His purpose.

"... warning them not to tell who he was. This was to fulfill what was spoken through the prophet Isaiah" (Matthew 12:16 - 17)

- When discussing the parable of the sower Jesus Himself declared:

"though seeing, they do not see; though hearing, they do not hear or understand. In them is fulfilled the prophecy of Isaiah" (Matthew 13:13 - 14)

While Jesus testified how they fulfilled Isaiah's prophecy, many more continue today to hear but not understand.

- After Jesus delivered a few of His parables He declared

"So was fulfilled what was spoken through the prophet: 'I will open my mouth in parables, I will utter things hidden since the creation of the world'." (Matthew 13:34 - 35)

- Just prior to Christ's entry into Jerusalem He sent two apostles ahead to retrieve a colt.

  "This took place to fulfill what was spoken through the prophet: 'Say to the Daughter of Zion, "See, your king comes to you, gentle and riding on a donkey, on a colt, the foal of a donkey."'" (Matthew 21:4)

See Zechariah 9:9 as it was first foretold.

- When Jesus was arrested He directed His companions to put their weapons away telling them that He could call upon His Father to save Him with thousands of angels "But how then would the Scriptures be fulfilled that say it must happen in this way?". Remember that in Matthew 5:17 He had earlier stated that He had come for a purpose—to fulfill the writings of the prophets. Jesus continues on to tell His accusers in that they could have arrested Him without their weapons every day in the temple courts

  "But this has all taken place that the writings of the prophets might be fulfilled." (Matthew 26:56)

- After Judas had betrayed Jesus and threw the 30 pieces of silver back at his fellow conspirators, they used the money to buy a burial place for foreigners.

  "Then what was spoken by Jeremiah the prophet was fulfilled. They took the thirty silver coins, the price set on him by the people of Israel ...". (Matthew 27:9)

Zechariah also described the betrayal amount as 30 pieces of silver in 11:12 - 13.

Still other examples can be found in the gospels of events that fulfilled the writings of the prophets. The preceding examples are but a taste of the evidence of the accuracy of prophecy when compared with the New Testament gospel of Matthew. I encourage you to read and see, to hear and believe, to accept and know all these things He awaits to share with His followers.

## Prophecy From the Very First Book

The first book of the Old Testament shows amazing accuracy in Abraham's response to Issac as they made their way up Mount Moriah and Issac asked "what will we sacrifice?" to which Abraham responded

"God himself will provide the lamb ...". Note that the lamb came later, 41 generations later in the form of His own Son, Jesus. As God planned it, Abraham's son was spared, which was "atraditional" in the land where they lived. Abraham would have conformed to a ritual of first born sacrifice until he broke that custom and returned down with his live son. Of course off in the bush was a ram; please note, not a lamb. And as God planned it, the Lamb of God, His own Son was the actual sacrifice almost two thousand years later.

Other similarities between Issac's aborted sacrifice and Christ's actual sacrifice including:

•   it was three days from the time Abraham was commanded to sacrifice Issac until Abraham's hand was withheld and in effect Issac's life restored, Jesus took three days to rise again to life;

•   Issac was laid on the wood, Jesus was laid on a wooden cross;

•   Abraham offered his only Son (per God's promise, see Genesis 22:2) as did the Father send His only son;

•   Issac walked away from his experience, Christ walked after His sacrifice;

•   Issac fulfilled a covenant God made to Abraham and Jesus fulfilled a new covenant made for man.

•   Even prior to Abraham's aborted sacrifice of Issac, God promised Abraham that "... all the peoples on earth will be blessed through you". This too happened when Jesus was offered as the atonement for the sins of all people. Its pronouncement was delivered 50 days later by Peter who declared salvation through Christ at the feast of Pentecost.

Of course many other prophecies concerning the life of Christ were foretold by the prophets and throughout the Old Testament. Some of the prophets, designated as the "minor" prophets were so depicted because of the shorter length of their books. Similarly, the books of Jeremiah, Ezekiel, and Isaiah were considered "major" due to the length of their writings. Even before the time of Christ these minor prophet writings were considered a single entity. However, these books were always considered to be equally inspired with the other works of Scripture.

Imagine yourself as the "minor" prophet Zechariah (previously referenced) or the "minor" prophet Micah writing

> "But you, Bethlehem Ephrathah, though you are small among the clans of Judah, out of you will come for me one who will be ruler over Israel, whose origins are from of old, from ancient times." (Micah 5:2)

Luke 2:4 - 6 describes this fulfillment of this prophecy over 700 years after it was written. What a marvelous prophecy to come through Micah. Hosea, another minor prophet writes

> "When Israel was a child, I loved him, and out of Egypt I called my son." (Hosea 11:1)

In Matthew 2:19 Joseph was told in a dream to return to Israel from Egypt to where he and his family had escaped Herod's persecution of all the young male infants and toddlers. Upon this return, Joseph, Mary, and Jesus settled in Nazareth, this too in fulfillment of the words of the prophets. I recommend a review of the NIV Study Bible notes on Matthew 2:23 for a summary of these prophecies.

The understanding of these verses and how they were perceived in Jesus' day is important. During the life of Christ, the people of Israel sought a political rescue from the coming Messiah, not a spiritual savior. Had they accepted the spiritual rescue Jesus offered, all their other needs would have been satisfied; but they did not recognize their Messiah because He didn't seem to fit their current needs. Jesus was rejected.

This lesson has real application in our lives today. I yearn not to miss or be unprepared for the second coming of Jesus. Imagine being back in the time of Christ, attending a Bible study (Old Testament necessarily) and discussing the current events of the day. Imagine questioning a fellow participant or even teacher about the uproar created by this man Jesus. Imagine one person in the Bible study arguing that this could not possibly be the Messiah because He needs to be called up from Egypt. Imagine a second person contending that the Messiah would be born in Bethlehem. Imagine a third retorting the necessity for the Messiah to be called a Nazarene. Imagine still a fourth throwing up his hands as saying "how could all these prophecies be true when they are all contradictory"? Don't we hear the same argument today, that there appear to be contradictions and or inconsistencies in God's Word? Are these statements made by those who study the Bible for understanding or merely to question its verses out of context? Do you read the Word with faith or do you examine it to reinforce doubt?

Of course today, with history and God's revelation we know there was no contradiction in the words of the prophets. Every prophecy was true and fulfilled exactly as foretold. Over 300 prophecies were fulfilled with the birth of Jesus. Only a few prophecies have been presented to merit your recognition of the Bible's truthfulness. I pray not to try to know so much about Him, that I miss knowing Him. I don't want to be unprepared to know Him spiritually as Israel once did; all else will be addressed through His provision. I don't want Him to come in accordance with my plan, I want to ensure that I come to Him in accordance with His plan!

Even Moses wrote under God's direction about the coming Christ some 1400 years prior to His birth. When God first called Abram (later to be called Abraham) He promised:

"I will bless those who bless you, and whoever curses you I will curse, and all peoples on earth will be blessed through you." (Genesis 12:3)

Matthew 1 and Luke 3 both describe the lineage from Abraham to Jesus. Through Jesus all peoples have grace available to them, a gift through which all nations have been blessed. Matthew 28:16 - 20, also known as the great commissioning, implores us to go into all the nations baptizing in the name of the Father, Son, and Holy Spirit. The resurrected Christ tells us something else of key importance in these verses. He says that all authority has been given unto Him confirming His domain and kingdom. These words reinforced the words delivered at His own baptism when the voice from heaven spoke saying "this is My Son in whom I love and with whom I am well pleased."

Jesus' statements confirm what the Psalmist wrote

"All the ends of the earth will remember and turn to the Lord, and all the families of the nations will bow down before him, for dominion belongs to the Lord and he rules over the nations.'" (Psalm 22:7)

Isaiah reiterates

"Before me every knee will bow; by me every tongue will swear." (Isaiah 45:23)

While these prophecies point toward the time of His second coming, many witnessed His power and dominion and majesty during His earthly ministry 2000 years ago. I find an extra measure of comfort with so many prophecies fulfilled and expressed by so many–from Abraham to David, to the prophets, and all the way to the last and most prophetic book of Scripture.

Other Psalms are quite prophetic in nature as well.

"I will open my mouth in parables, I will utter hidden things, things from of old." (Psalm 78:2)

Jesus spoke in parables all throughout the synoptic gospels. Parables were a primary teaching vehicle for Jesus. The consistency of Jesus' message through parables in the Bible testifies to its accuracy, overall purpose, theme, and divine nature.

God's covenant is prophesied further in Genesis 17:19 when God told a one hundred year old man that his 90 year old wife would have a child through whom an everlasting covenant would be established. Even Sarah scoffed at the whole idea as silly when she first heard it, because of her age. It was also unlikely that well beyond child-bearing years she might have her first child. Again, both Matthew and Luke identify Issac as Abraham's son. Did God wait for Abraham and Sarah to be so far beyond their years to have a child so as to demonstrate that He can do anything, or so that we would begin to understand His faithfulness or His promises?

Jesus' birth was foretold by the prophet Isaiah when he was told

"The virgin will be with child and will give birth to a son, and will call him Immanuel." (Isaiah 7:14)

Matthew 1:21 describes Joseph's dream wherein he is told to name the child Jesus because He will save His people from their sins, not the political forces of the Roman empire of that day. Matthew 1:22 - 23 confirms that these events took place to fulfill the writings of the prophet about 700 years earlier.

Continuing on in Isaiah Chapter 53 are numerous prophecies about how Jesus would be treated, abused, rejected, wounded, and cutoff even though He would not be violent nor spoke any deceit. The chapter concludes with why these events would take place "for he bore the sin of many, and made intercession for the transgressors." (Isaiah 53:11)

He died even for those who would kill Him. The gospels are filled with the evidence of these prophecies and not only the gospels but the records of the Roman empire and the documents of non-sympathetic historians of that day.

## Some Prophecies Concerning the Nation of Israel

One of the most amazingly accurate prophecies of the Old Testament came from the prophet Daniel. Daniel was recognized as a prophet of God even though he never held the official position of prophet in his native homeland. Daniel spent almost his entire life in Babylon during the exile of the Jews. This is the Daniel who survived a night in the lion's den only to have his accusers gobbled up by the same lions after his night ended. Daniel is the same Daniel who interpreted Nebuchadnezzar's dreams and prophesied the king's loss of supremacy. Nebuchadnezzar was later reinstated after accepting and praising the true God. Daniel is the same Daniel who read the "writing on the wall" for Belshazzar and whose kingdom was taken from him even that night. That invasion of the Medes and capture of the magnificent and well-fortified city of Babylon is still held against the Jews by Iraq. The invasion of the Medes (Persians and modern day Iran) and the downfall of the Babylonian empire, continues to be a source of resentment by Iraq. No doubt an incentive for why Saddam Hussein redirected his missiles during the Iraqi conflict in 1991.

Daniel has an incredible track record for prophecy. Daniel specifically states

"Know and understand this: From the issuing of the decree to restore and rebuild Jerusalem until the Anointed One, the ruler, comes, there will be seven 'sevens', and sixty-two sevens. It will be rebuilt with streets and a trench, but in times of trouble. After the sixty-two 'sevens', the Anointed One will be cut off and will have nothing. The people of the ruler who will come will destroy the city and the sanctuary ...".
(Daniel 9:25 - 26)

While the reader is encouraged to research and validate the offered meaning of the 'sevens' described by Daniel, the 'sevens' are translated weeks of years' with each week being seven years. The people of the ruler who was to come were the Romans; this indicates that the Antichrist will also arise out of the reassembled former Roman Empire.

Daniel, who began to understand the prophecy about the 70 year exile prophesied by Jeremiah (25:11) to the year, and knowing the accuracy of God's promises sought God in prayer to reveal His purpose for His chosen people. On March 14, 445 BC, as determined by the Royal Observatory in Greenwich, Persian King Artazerxes Longimanus (in the twentieth year of his reign and on the first day of Nisan per Nehemiah 2:1), issued a decree that allowed the rebuilding of Jerusalem.

Now back to Daniel's 'seven' and sixty-two 'sevens' or sixty-nine 'weeks of years.' Sixty-nine multiplied by seven (weeks of years) is 483 years. The Biblical month is first found in Genesis during the flood of Noah's time. The Biblical year is confirmed throughout and then conclusively in the end of the Bible in Revelation where three and one-half years, forty-two months, and 1260 days are used to describe the same time period, a 360 day year. Multiplying 360 by 483 results in a sum of 173,880 days. Daniel prophesied that the Messiah would be cutoff after these 173,880 days had passed. Continuing with the mathematics, adding 173,880 days to March 14, 445 BC brings us to April 6, 32 AD. April 6, 32 AD is the day recognized as the first Palm Sunday.

That first Palm Sunday was Israel's day of visitation by the Messiah. He was rejected and cutoff by the people thereby fulfilling to the exact day Daniel's prophesy. As the apostle Luke recalls the words of Jesus

> "As he approached Jerusalem and saw the city, he wept over it and said, If you, even you, had only known on this day what would bring you peace—but now it is hidden from your eyes. The days will come upon you when your enemies will build an embankment against you and encircle you and hem you in on every side. They will dash you to the ground, you and the children within your walls. They will not leave one stone on another, because you did not recognize the time of God's coming to you." (Luke 19:41 - 44)

I prefer the King James Version for the last phrase "thou knewest not the time of thy visitation". Reread Daniel 9:26 for further emphasis and fuller appreciation of the absolute accuracy of the Scriptures.

What's equally shocking is that this information is not new. I first read its details in Grant Jeffrey's <u>Armageddon Appointment with Destiny</u> [1]. In this excellent book on prophecy fulfilled and yet to be fulfilled, Mr. Jeffrey reports the investigative skills of a former head of Scotland Yard--a Sir Robert Anderson who penned the details of his study almost 100 years ago in his book <u>The Coming Prince</u>. We are more likely to remember the name Jack the Ripper on whose case Sir Anderson reportedly worked than the tremendous understanding he bequeathed of God's prophetic and accurate Word! These intriguing events are also summarized in the Stewart and Missler's <u>The Coming Temple</u> [2].

The writings of both Daniel and Isaiah have been found to be so historically accurate that many who oppose the veracity of the Bible as a whole, claim that they could not possibly have been written prior to the events they prophesy. Daniel 11:1 - 35 is said to be supported by 135 events fulfilled since its writing. Those critics who discount these early writings have little regard for an almighty and all knowing God who is in complete control. This same God is our God of hope and salvation.

Bible critics may also be unaware of the contents of the Dead Sea Scrolls. Modern day findings like the Dead Sea Scrolls, found between 1947 and the early 1950s, illustrate the remarkable accuracy with which Scripture has been copied. These 800 scrolls, dated not later than 200 BC, contain pieces of every Old Testament book except Esther. These scrolls include the book of Daniel wherein copies of Daniel's message from as early as 600 BC were being copied; some before and some after the events they described. Some of these scrolls are available to the viewing public in Israel; still others have been closely held by a small number of scholars.

The good news/bad news aspects of Daniel's prophecies need to be identified. The bad news is that we won't live to see the prophecy of the 69 weeks just described--they have already occurred. The good news is that Daniel prophesied the coming of the Antichrist in his last "week" (seven) of years. This time is yet to come; it directly precedes Christ's second coming. I believe that this time is so near that to postpone the writing of this book would be irresponsible. The closeness of Christ's second coming is a strong motivation for completing this book in a timely fashion. Now more than ever is the time for each of us, as encouraged through Scripture, to study the Scripture, to use the

Scriptures as the source of truth, to abandon man's way of doing "stuff" and accept His Word; no other gospels, no add-ons, and no traditions, that replace or contradict His plan.

Another prophet, a contemporary of Daniel's was the priest Ezekiel. Ezekiel was also exiled to Babylon and also had an amazingly accurate prophecy. Ezekiel's prophecy tells us a great deal about the current nation of Israel. In addition, this prophecy describes why the people of Israel have been punished for so long.

I have heard noted ministers confess that they cannot tell you why the Jews have suffered so over the years. I can remember reenacting the passion in the Catholic church on more than once occasion. The priest would play the role of Pontius Pilate and the congregation the people choosing the release between Jesus and Barabbas. In response to the priest's question "What should I do, then, with the one you call the king of the Jews?" as quoted from Mark 15:12, I can recall the congregation, acting as the crowd in Jesus' day, shouting "crucify him". Somehow, I could not bring myself to repeat those words.

Pilate knew the injustice being perpetrated and he washed his hands of the mockery telling the people "it's your responsibility." Luke describes how Pilate appealed to the people three times. Unfortunately the people responded "Let his blood be on us and on our children" and in John's account "We have no king but Caesar." What an awful tragedy the Father must have felt when His own son was rejected, even though He knew what was to happen.

So many of the parables which Jesus used to teach His disciples dealt with rejection. If we could only see today what was overlooked then. As God's chosen people and nation, after the glory He shone upon them, after the miracles Jesus worked for them, Israel should have known their king.

But another reason may be evidenced for the treatment of the Jews over the past two thousand years. As Grant Jeffrey discovered in <u>Armageddon Appointment with Destiny</u> God prophesied the rebirth of Israel precisely as it occurred on May 14, 1948, through the words of the prophet Ezekiel. Ezekiel was told:

> "Then lie on your left side and put the sin of the house of Israel upon yourself. You are to bear their sin for the number of days you lie on your side. I have assigned you the same number of days as the years of their sin. So for 390 days you

will bear the sin of the house of Israel. After you have finished this, lie down again, this time on your right side, and bear the sin of the house of Judah. I have assigned you 40 days, a day for each year." (Ezekiel 4:4 - 6)

A very clear message from this Scripture is a year of punishment for a day of lying; a total of 430 years. We have seen from Daniel's prophecy that 70 years were spent in exile in Babylon; these years because Israel refused to honor the Sabbath and ignored God's command that they love Him only. In reality, they were told to enter the land they were promised by Him. They were told to destroy all its inhabitants, accept no customs, nor intermarry, otherwise the people of Israel could fall victim to accepting the pagan worship practices already in the lands they were to inherit. Deuteronomy 7 clearly states what the people were to do.

In contrast, falsely believing the ways of man could improve the ways of God, the Jews allowed the earlier occupants of the land to coexist-exist. Eventually both groups intermarried. Eventually, the children of God built altars to the pagans. Even the wisest man and the wealthiest man ever to live, Solomon, shared in being disobedient.

The people of Israel refused to keep the Sabbath holy; to give the land its Sabbath rest. The Sabbath rest required that the land be rested every seventh year. Leviticus 26 begins

"Do not make idols or set up an image or a sacred stone for yourselves, and do not place a carved stone in your land to bow down before it. I am the Lord your God. Observe my Sabbaths and have reverence for my sanctuary. I am the Lord." (Leviticus 26:1)

Leviticus 26:14 includes the penalties for disobedience. In verse 17

"I will set my face against you so that you will be defeated by your enemies; those who hate you will rule over you, and you will flee even when no one is pursuing you. If after all this you will not listen to me, I will punish you for your sins *seven times over*. I will break down your stubborn pride." (Leviticus 26:17 - 19a, emphasis mine)

And in verse 21

"I will multiply your afflictions *seven times over,* as your sins deserve." (Leviticus 26:21 NIV, emphasis mine)

And finally in verse 24

> "I myself will be hostile toward you and will afflict you for
> your sins *seven times over.*" (Leviticus 26:24 NIV, emphasis
> mine)

These verses are also quite specific about the further punishment that
would befall the Israelites if their disobedience continued. History
confirms that verse 17 occurred, and the Israelites were exiled to
Babylon for seventy years.

Remember that Ezekiel had been told to lie on his side for a total of 430
days. Even though the Israelites were free to return to Jerusalem after
the Babylonian empire, only about ten percent actually did. The rest
stayed and continued in the customs of their captors. Multiplying seven
(the seven times over) by the remaining 360 years (Biblical year) is a
total of 2520 Biblical years. Now if the nation of Israel had to be
reestablished anywhere within 10 years of this calculation I would have
been impressed. Considering that Israel was destroyed in 70 AD, its
future was tenuous at best. If such a prophecy came within one year of
fulfillment it would be incredible. But the reality is that May 14, 1948,
was 2520 Biblical years, (seven times 360 years) from 536 BC the year
Cyrus allowed the children of Israel to return from exile in Babylon.
See Mr. Jeffrey's book for a more complete review of this fulfillment.

More recently, the returning of Jews from the Soviet Union fulfills
another prophecy wherein God promises in the last days to return them
to their homeland from the nation to the north. The parable of the fig
tree described in Matthew, and the symbolic use of the fig tree
(Jeremiah 24) to represent Israel in the Old Testament is another vivid
message concerning the times in which we live.

In summary, the Israelites returned to idols, they made images with their
hands and bowed down to them doing precisely what they were told not
to do, and they ignored God's commands in regard to the Sabbath. They
did not heed the judgment they received in Babylon, they continued in
their sinful ways, and they unknowingly handed their own Messiah over
to the Gentiles to be put to death. It is understandable from a Scriptural
perspective why they have suffered. But don't count the Israelites out,
they will always be God's people and those who bless them, God will
bless; those who curse them, God will curse. Our own country must
recognize these evident Biblical truths in all areas of foreign policy;
especially in peace negotiations in the Middle East. Perhaps we can

also understand the root of one's reluctance to holler in unison with the congregation "crucify Him." That's our Savior, being crucified for each of us. We must learn from history and not repeat, even symbolically, the wickedness of man; choosing rather to concentrate of the atonement of His sacrifice.

## Brief Archaeological Evidence and Scripture

Over the past several thousand years, which would you guess was rewritten: Biblical accounts of worldly events or the history books regarding worldly events. The Bible has not been rewritten to reflect current or apparent archaeological evidence. Let's examine just a few events to further reinforce our belief in the absolute accuracy of Scripture.

Before establishing the following series of comments with evidence, I must admit a preference that no one adopt my understanding or value system as a replacement for their own Scriptural exegesis. It's "a lost blessing" for anyone who might use my thoughts to shape their vision on an omnipotent God. Each person needs to make the connection between Scripture and salvation on their own account. The following examples serve to stimulate an interest through which one may discover God's message for himself. This message will not deviate from Scripture. An acid test of one's understanding is conformance to Scripture.

Numerous authors and scientists support a worldwide flood. Scientists dispute among themselves any question that could have more than one possible outcome; therefore, all will not agree. Recent topological changes as a result of the Mount St. Helen's eruptions have reignited age-old debates. Did it really take hundreds of thousands or millions of years for the Grand Canyon to be formed? Can life return to a devastated area so quickly? How many eruptions would be needed to darken the earth substantially and for a sustained period to bring the dinosaurs to extinction?

Everyone will not agree to disregard the value of science when it is used to contradict Scripture. Egyptian history books describe the accounts of the afflictions imposed by God because of Pharaoh's hardened heart. Science cannot explain how it hailed on the Egyptians but not on the Jews, or how it was dark in all of Egypt except the area inhabited by the Jews. The cloud that led the Jews out of Egypt by day, and the pillar of fire by night could be discounted as a tornado or brilliance from a far off volcanic eruption. Scientifically, the Red Sea could not part and allow the exiled Jews to walk on dry land—a land, which a short time later returned to sea and swallowed the Egyptians. The Jordan also parted when the Ark of the Covenant passed through it. But that cannot be explained by science either. Science cannot describe how the sun went backwards or how days were lengthened during battles over the promised land, both in response to prayer. Instead some scientists attempt to theorize away reality by conjuring stories that are even more remarkable than the biblical events they purport to explain.

Geisler and Brooks examine archaeological evidence for both the Old and New Testaments in their book When Skeptics Ask [3]. In this book they quote an Egyptian priest named Ipuwer who documented the impact of the plagues. They examine other topics like the flood, the Tower of Babel, the writings of Moses, the amazing fulfillment of the prophecy of the destruction of Tyre, the Babylonian captivity, and other evidences of Christ's life by secular historians. These materials are well researched and include several references for further study.

Halley's Bible Handbook [4] is a condensed source of archaeological evidence for the accuracy of Scripture. This book, in addition to being a source of Biblical insight, overviews discoveries, the Dead Sea Scrolls, and places from the Bible. Examples include: the flood of Noah's time that is referenced in Babylonian accounts; the destruction of the prophets of Baal by Elijah after discovering jars containing infant remains from idol sacrifices; and how history in 1853 first acknowledged Belshazzar of one of the Babylonian kings with whom Daniel dealt. This first appendix has over 100 references. His second appendix lists over 70 places that provide the archaeological evidence to support the writings of Scripture. Other references in the Bibliography will assist the interested reader in proving beyond any and all reasonable doubt that the Bible says what it says because it is unquestionably correct.

## When Science Meets Scripture

A fascinating culmination of research and evidence has been accumulated by Dr. D. Russell Humphreys. This work should be examined by the scientists who tend to date the earth's life in the billions of years. Dr. Humphreys presents materials that conflict with a multi-billion year evolution of the universe. While confiding that further arguments support "Evidence for a Young Universe," the paper I have summarizes fifteen arguments. A few are reiterated below.

1. About 450 million tons of sodium are deposited into the oceans each year. Less than 125 million tons escape. At that rate, if the oceans been without any sodium in the beginning, only 42 million years would have been required to reach current sodium levels. Such an aging period is far less than the 3 or 4 billion year age sometimes attributed to the earth.

2. Trees found in multiple fossil layers had to have been formed in less than a few years; that is, buried faster than the decay rate. Evolutionary theory holds that the top and bottom layers were developed over millions of years.

3. Geological evidence supports the likelihood that events surrounding the formation of the Cambrian Sawatch sandstone occurred just hundreds of years apart from each other. This evidence is contrary to the theory that the sandstone west of Colorado Springs, in the Ute Pass fault was formed over a 500 million year span of time.

4. The absence of skeletons and other buried artifacts from the 100,000 year stone age, at a time when populations were believed to be between one and ten million would have yielded over four billion sets of remains. Only a few thousand have been found suggesting a stone age of a few hundred years.

5. The beginning of written records about 5000 years ago implies while prehistoric man was capable of art, engineering, and astronomy, man kept no written records for 95,000 years.

Dr. Humphreys is a physicist at a large national laboratory in Albuquerque, New Mexico. His work is thoroughly documented and draws extensively on the efforts of his fellow scientists.

Finally, additional resources are available from the "Institute for Creation Research" whose central focus is to present the evidence of God's plan for creation.

This discussion of Biblical accuracy is intentionally curtailed in order to dedicate more time and space to accomplish the original purpose of this work—to glorify the Father by leading others to His Word, truth, and a walk in obedience. Timothy states it succinctly

"Do your best to present yourself to God as one approved, a workman who does not need to be ashamed and who correctly handles the word of truth." (2 Timothy 2:15)

I am unaware who made the following popular quotation: "Those who are down on the Bible are not up on the Bible." About 25 percent of the Bible is prophetic in nature. The Bible contains 31,124 verses. Simple mathematics implies over than 3000 prophetic verses, more than half of which have already been fulfilled. No single archaeological finding has ever disproved a single word of the Bible.

## The Bible–Taking It Personally

Hal Lindsey deserves the credit for stimulating my early interest in the Bible through his book The Late Great Planet Earth. Great as his book was and as much interest as it stirred in me I was unable to recognize Christ's conditional plan of salvation and His unconditional forgiveness. I believe God interceded directly in my life several times prior to my understanding of His forgiveness, but as least twice in response to specific prayer.

On July 19, 1982, our first child was born and we named him Joshua. We did not intend that he be named the most popular boy's name of 1982. Originally we wanted to name him Jeremiah but we finally settled on Joshua. Nor did we know at the time Joshua most closely matched the name by which Jesus was called. Jesus is the Greek translation of the Hebrew Yeshua. Lastly, we did not know the Joshua in Exodus, was originally named Hoshea before Moses changed his named from meaning "salvation" to "the Lord is salvation." All things considered, I am happy with our choice.

In any case, I can remember experiencing the miracle of birth for the first time. Wow! It was great and I did not intend to allow my masculinity to hide the tears that streamed down my cheeks. I have friends who discount the miracle of life because of its "commonness." I now know children are a reward from the Lord (Psalm 127:3). Perhaps we mistake His generosity because He has made life so common and good for us.

I remember even prior to Joshua's birth, committing to changing my lifestyle to reduce the opportunity for me to set a bad example for my children. My wife and I became regular church attendees. We missed less than a handful of Sunday services in the past ten years. By contrast, we probably attended Sunday services less than a handful of times in the ten years prior to that period.   We can now look back and be grateful that God provided us the time and the renewed interest to read His Word: Revelation, then the New Testament, and then the Old Testament.   It became a commitment to read the Old or New Testament on alternating years during the Catholic period of Lent.   While having made that journey several times, each reading facilitated greater learning, understanding, and belief.   The real benefit of having read the Scriptures, over and over on my own, was the chance to develop a personal relationship with God through the Scriptures.   Examining the Scriptures produced an unexpected effect.   Many of the traditions of the Catholic church seemed to have been missing.   Examples include:

*   no mention of purgatory,

*   no mention of Mary's assumption (even though the New Testament covers well beyond her death),

*   no praying to or intervention by saints (the word saints is used in the Bible to represent those saved in Christ not those nominated by a church),

*   no praying by Jesus to Mary or saints (in fact the prayer He taught His disciples was the Our Father),

*   no mention of rosaries (described by other researchers as an adopted Hindu practice),

*   no mention of the use of scapulars for salvation (or other medals) although there are several Scriptural references forbidding the making of any image for worship or faith

Being somewhat concerned about the apparent discrepancies, both numerous and consequential, I began to feel some discomfort.   I remember being visited by the Jehovah Witnesses and their open criticism of altars and crosses.   They used Scripture to substantiate their position.   I read their materials and decided it was not quite what I thought the Bible taught.   Subsequent materials confirmed my initial uneasiness with the Jehovah Witnesses although I appreciated their sincerity and willingness to reach those they thought lost.

I began to study different religions, their formations, doctrines, prophecies, and current beliefs.   Nothing else I studied seemed to compare favorably with the accuracy, consistency, and love for all men as found in the Bible.   I continue to use the term "Bible" recognizing that several other religious groups also have a book that many of them refer to as their bible. The Bible to which I testify is the one that begins with Genesis, ends with Revelation, contains 66 books, and 31,124 verses.

I noticed here were certain things I began to withdraw from during the Sacrifice of the Mass. Singing hymns to Mary, stating the phrase "one Holy Catholic and apostolic church", and questioning other traditions became the rule rather than the exception.

Running was one of my favorite therapeutic and physical conditioning pastimes. Music filled a void during runs that exceeded an hour. I'd run daily, without failure and at one point was within three months of having run daily for five years without missing a day. I terminated that streak in an effort to improve my power lifting; another activity used to fill my spare time. Looking back I remember meeting "Christian powerlifters." I do not remember being "tuned in" to the Christian message.

Running on Sundays was a little challenging in that there was rarely any good music I could receive on the frugal radio I carried. Usually, for the sake of company, I would listen to whatever was on. Occasionally, and then habitually, I listed to a Dr. Bruce Dunn. Of course initially I listened tentatively—he was after all a Presbyterian, a Protestant. What this man preached though usually made a lot of sense (the rest of the time I probably didn't understand him). In 1991 Dr. Dunn celebrated 40 years of Bible-based teaching. I've listened to him for at least the last ten years and still look forward to his message at 7:00 a.m. on Sundays. Thank God for preachers who teach from the Word of God; Dr. Dunn is surely one of them.

| Three things you should know after reading this chapter. |
| --- |

✟  Jesus loves you. Even before you knew Him, He knew you. Even before you accept Him, He loves you. Whether you know Him or if you still need to know Him, He loves you every bit as much.

✟  Jesus seeks a relationship with you. Can you imagine withholding your time and company from someone who loves you? We need the ongoing relationship with God that He wants to have with each of us. Jesus laid down His own life for us so that we could spend eternity with Him. Establish or reopen your account with Him today.

✞ Jesus wants you to love your brothers. Fellowship with the Lord. Devoting yourself to His Word and principles leads to fellowship with other believers; sharing in their burdens and in their joys. The joy of the Lord is something you can always give away and yet never deplete.

References

[1] Grant R. Jeffrey, Armageddon Appointment with Destiny, Bantam Books

[2] Don Stewart and Chuck Missler, The Coming Temple, Dart Press, 1991

[3] Norman L. Geisler and Ronald M. Brooks, When Skeptics Ask, Victor Books

Other Suggested Readings

Dave Breese, Know the Mark of Cults, Victor Books, 1979

D. Russell Humphreys; "Evidence for a Young Universe;" Creation Science Fellowship of New Mexico, Inc.; November, 1992

*I pray not to try to know so much about Him,*

*that I miss knowing Him.*

*I don't want to be unprepared to know Him spiritually as Israel once did;*

*all else will be addressed through His provision.*

# Chapter 2

# Tradition: Its Origins and the Catholic Church

A friend of mine greatly enjoys doing character-based Bible studies. What he shares is valuable. Others tend to develop a better understanding of Biblical concepts by doing word studies - or Word studies. This second approach can be applied to the word "tradition" as found throughout the Word.

The first use of the word "tradition" in the New Testament is found in Matthew as the Pharisees asked:

> "'Why do your disciples break the traditions of the elders? They don't wash their hands before they eat!' Jesus replied, 'And why do you break the command of God for the sake of your tradition?'" (Matthew 15:2 - 3)

Not only had the Pharisees established their own traditions, but Jesus' response clearly indicates the Pharisees had gone a step too far; they replaced His commands with their own teachings.

Tradition is a fundamental teaching of the Catholic church. Doctrinally, tradition is considered by the Catholic church to be of equal authority with Scripture per the yet prevailing doctrines of the Council of Trent. Verse 6 continues

> "' ... Thus you nullify the word of God for the sake of your tradition.'" (Matthew 15:6)

Is it possible that modern day Pharisees commit the same mistake? The next use of the word tradition occurs in Mark's version of apparently the same incident.

> "He replied, 'Isaiah was right when he prophesied about you hypocrites; as it is written: '"These people honor me with their lips, but their hearts are far from me. They worship me in vain; their teachings are but rules taught by men." You have let go of the commands of God and are holding on to the traditions of men.' And he said to them: 'You have a fine way of setting aside the commands of God in order to observe your own traditions!'" (Mark 7:6 - 9)

Finishing with verse 13

> "Thus you nullify the word of God by your tradition that you have handed down. And you do many things like that." (Mark 7:13)

Jesus provided a number of insights with these verses.

1. He affirmed the authenticity of Isaiah's writings.

2. He demonstrated the reading and recitation of Scripture was important for He, Himself, knew the Scriptures.

3. He described the behavior of the Pharisees as hypocritical. Some of the strongest words Jesus used were directed at hypocrites. Seven woes are issued to the same hypocrites in Matthew. Also in Matthew, Christ warns against hypocritical judgment.

4. He describes how the Pharisees are hypocrites: their words don't match their hearts.

5. He evaluates the effectiveness of their prayer - "they worship me in vain".

6. He tells them what they are doing wrong - letting go of God's commands while holding onto man's tradition.

7. He provides a motive - in order to observe your own traditions. This practice attempts to put man on par with God. Eve too once thought her actions would lead to being equal with God.

8. He tells them that the net effect is to nullify His word. This abrogation includes His promises, rewards, and love as well.

9. He warns them that they do many things like this - substituting their ways for His way.

Many lessons exist in Mark's account of this exchange.

The next use of the word tradition is in Colossians.

> "See to it that no one takes you captive through hollow and deceptive philosophy, which depends on human tradition and the basic principles of this world rather than on Christ."
> (Colossians 2:8)

These words in Paul's letter warn the Colossians of events beginning to take place even in the times of the early church. The words "hollow" and "deceptive" paint a picture of emptiness and illusion. These words are consistent with Christ's in Matthew and Mark.

The King James Version [1] of the Bible uses the word "tradition" in Thessalonians although the NIV uses the word teaching.

> "... keep away from every brother who is idle and does not live according to the teaching you received from us."
> (2 Thessalonians 3:6)

Paul's teachings were not contrary to Christ's. Any "teaching" would have been consistent therefore with Jesus'. Paul did not replace the teachings of Scripture with the teachings of man. Instead, he encouraged these readers to receive the teachings whether passed on by word of mouth or letter (2 Thessalonians 2:15). The New Testament had not yet been completed and published, although the gospels and letters were being widely circulated. Paul did not encourage the Thessalonians to develop their own traditions.

First Peter is the next reference wherein "tradition" is used in the King James Version.

> "Forasmuch as ye know that ye were not redeemed with corruptible things, as silver and gold, from your vain conversation received by tradition from your fathers;"
> (1 Peter 1:18)

The wording, not the meaning is slightly different in the NIV. Nonetheless, Peter declares tradition did not rescue his readers from their empty life; tradition could not, they needed Christ the Sacrificial Lamb.

The word "traditions" is referenced in two places in the New Testament in the NIV. The first was examined above in the episode in Mark 7 where "traditions is found in verses 4, 8 and 9. The second reference is in Galatians.

"I was advancing in Judaism beyond many Jews of my own age and was extremely zealous for the traditions of my father." (Galatians 1:14)

Paul later describes how God changed all that, thereby discounting the value of the tradition.

This completes an all inclusive review of the words "tradition" and "traditions" as used in the Scriptures. Can you sense a distinct distrust for tradition, the substituted ways that seem right to a man but, as Proverbs 14:12 and 16:25 describe "leads unto death"? I believe the substitution of tradition in place of Scripture is another one of man's fruitless attempts to tell God what His plan would look like if He had been as smart as us!

I believe that the substitution of tradition in place of Scripture is another one of man's fruitless attempts to tell God what His plan would have looked like if He had only been as smart as us!

Despite the prior review of traditions as described throughout the Bible, the Catholic church's position on tradition is that it is of equal authority with Scripture. This stand has allowed the infiltration of most of the Catholic traditions practiced today - so many of which contradict His commands and actions. Most Catholics are unaware that these traditions lack root in Biblical doctrine. Perhaps more alarming is due to the Catholic church's teachings, wherein many of its members have no understanding of God's plan of salvation. It has been lost and diluted by supplanted tradition. The Catholic church feels so strongly that it has final earthly authority that it has declared its own tradition equal with Scripture and curses anyone who does not endorse this dogma. This doctrine was formally published in an Article of Faith by the Council of Trent in 1545. This council and all of its doctrines are endorsed explicitly by the Second Vatican Council even though the Catholic church claims to have made substantial changes towards non-Catholics at the Second Vatican Council. This doctrine carries equally dire consequences for Catholics who may not endorse it. The Council of Trent was not shy in issuing anathemas, or curses, as part of its proceedings.  Over 100 curses were issued and many others will be examined in this book.

The New American Bible, the Catholic Edition, [2] discloses

"The Catholic church derives all of its teaching authority from its tradition, the doctrine which has come down to it from Christ.  This tradition is preserved in written form in the "Bible" which contains the principle truths of faith taught to the Apostles by Christ."

By its own admission, the Catholic church derives its authority from "tradition."  The description goes further though to reveal still another insight; the Bible contains the principle truths.  Actually, the Bible contains all the truth that man needs for a personal relationship with Christ our Lord.  Here's how Paul reminded the Colossians of the value of worldly principles:

"Since you died with Christ to the basic principles of this world, why, as though you still belonged to it, do you submit to its rules. "Do not handle!  Do not taste!  Do not touch!"?  These are all destined to perish with use, because they are based on human commands and teachings."
(Colossians 2:20 - 22)

If we add tradition to the Scripture, we may need someone else to interpret the Scripture in light of the tradition.  This intercession is how the Catholic church derives its purpose; as the mediator between man and God.  Examples include: who can baptize, who forgives sin, who can offer sacrifices to and for the dead, and who is capable of understanding and interpreting Scripture.  This teaching authority is self-fulfilling but contrary to Biblical teaching.  First Timothy 2:5 describes who the mediator is—and that is Christ Himself.  He alone is the all sufficient mediator.

Why should we use Scripture as the basis for teaching and understanding?  Why not supplement its "principles" with up-to-date information based on the world we have come to know?  Second Timothy provides a straight-forward answer

"All Scripture is God-breathed and is useful for teaching, rebuking, correcting and training in righteousness, so that the man of God may be equipped for every good work."
(2 Timothy 3:16)

From this pivotal Bible verse come several fundamental truths about the Scripture. First, all of Scripture comes from God. Second, it is useful for instilling the things of God (teaching and training). Third, it is useful for confronting things not of God (rebuking and correcting). We need a few more John the Baptists today; a few more voices in the wilderness. We need a few more calls for repentance. We are taught when Christ comes it will be just as in the days of Noah and Lot regarding the sinful nature of man. Fourth, the Scripture is intended for the man of God; that is, Scripture is of little value to the man who seeks not God nor His ways. Fifth, the purpose of Scripture is to equip us for both the glory of God and the salvation of man; to put Scripture to use in our own lives and to share it with others. These are some of the reasons Scripture is important to Christians; particularly as revealed in the above verse.

Recall the statement from earlier, "The Catholic church derives all of its teaching authority from its tradition." Let's examine some Old and New Testament passages regarding God's instructions related to His Word. Deuteronomy is a good place to begin.

"Do not add to what I command you and do not subtract from it, but keep the commands of the Lord your God that I give you." (Deuteronomy 4:2)

The tribes of Israel were told not to tamper with God's directives. Do not take anything away from it, and just as important - do not add anything to it! DO NOT ADD anything to it! DO NOT ADD anything to it!

Deuteronomy repeats the same message.

"See that you do all I command you; do not add to it or take away from it." (Deuteronomy 12:32)

Adam and Eve thought they could alter God's plan by just one tree. They, too, thought they could improve God's own plan. They, too, thought they could be more like Him but they used disobedience as their tool and selfishness as their motive.

Even the wisest man to ever live, Solomon, understood the truth of the Scripture. In Proverbs he instructs us

"Do not add to His words, or he will rebuke you and prove you a liar." (Proverbs 30:6)

Earlier we examined the writings of Peter and Paul from the New Testament to reveal Christ-inspired words on tradition and new teachings. The apostle John wrote a number of times about the teaching we should receive or rebuke. Discernment in teaching is addressed in John's first epistle in verse 2:24 and it is reinforced in his second.

> "Anyone who runs ahead and does not continue in the teaching of Christ does not have God; whoever continues in the teaching has both the Father and the Son." (2 John 9 - 11)

Does the Catholic church teach the teachings of Christ? Did Christ teach that any man was perfect in judgment (the pope)? Did Christ teach that any person was sinless (Mary)? Did Christ teach that any man could forgive sins (a priest)? Did Christ teach to abstain from certain foods (Lent)? Did Christ teach that we should pray to saints? Did Christ teach tradition over Scripture (Catholic doctrine)? Did Christ teach sacraments as requirements to salvation (Catholic doctrine)? Did Christ teach perpetual sacrifice for our atonement (the Sacrifice of the Mass)? Did Christ teach the adornment of statues and images and scapulars as having special power or influence in the Christian's life (Catholic doctrine)? These examples are add-ons to God's Word. These add-ons are just as disobedient as Adam and Eve's disobedience. The consequence of these add-ons is far more catastrophic. The add-ons of the Catholic church lead its believers outside God's will and plan. The Jews were also reminded of the likelihood of becoming like the pagans and manufacturing their own gods and their own salvation in Deuteronomy.

> "... so that you do not become corrupt and make for yourselves an idol, an image of any shape, whether formed like a man or a woman, or like any animal on earth or any bird that flies in the air, or like any creature that moves along the ground or any fish in the waters below. And when you look up to the sky and see the sun, the moon and the stars - all the heavenly array - do not be enticed into bowing down to them and worshiping things the Lord your God has apportioned to all the nations under heaven." (Deuteronomy 4:16 - 20)

In these verses are a few key concepts. The first is the act—make no image. Is the crucifix an image? Is the host an image? Are statues images? Are the stations of the cross images? The second is the purpose—so that you do not become corrupt. Is the making of images disobedience?  Is the attention directed at images (saints, Mary, events) deterring our concentration on Him?  The third is the motive–make for yourselves.  Is what we make for Him or for us?  Is what we make pleasing to Him or pleasing to the enemy?  Is what we make fortifying His kingdom or unlocking doors to another kingdom?

Let us gain encouragement and direction from the words Paul sent to Timothy.

> "If anyone teaches false doctrines and does not agree to the sound instruction of our Lord Jesus Christ and to godly teaching, he is conceited and understands nothing." (1 Timothy 6:3)

The preceding Scripture verses were taken from both the Old and the New Testaments.  Did Jesus Himself ever provide guidance on prayer?  When Jesus taught the apostles how to pray, it was in response to their request.  Jesus taught us specifically whom we are to serve and worship.  This passage is one of three rebukes the Lord uses in response to the devil when tempted three times after 40 days of fasting in the desert.  The devil offered Jesus great rewards if the Lord would just worship the devil.  Luke captures this lesson for us.

> "Jesus answered, 'It is written: "Worship the Lord your God and serve him only"'." (Luke 4:8)

The devil is still offering rewards today.  Today's rewards are not very different; including power, wealth, and authority.  The same rewards may be the result of God's grace or their source may be from the deceiver himself.  These same rewards may be present at our moments of greatest need or our moments of greatest weakness.  Certainly the devil thought Christ was at a pinnacle of weakness, both physically and spiritually, after His 40 days in the desert.  Let's remain vigilant and recognize that during our moments of weakness Satan may work to move our eyes off Christ and onto another object.  Let us seek instead to understand all things through Christ Jesus, taking every thought captive in obedience to Him (2 Corinthians 10:5).

## The Returning Christ–No Babe in a Manger

Someone once observed that armies (nations) are best prepared to fight the battle (war) they just lost.  In many respects some Christians are the same way. Because Jesus came to us as a babe in a manger, many folks are relying on a gentle, loving, and kind savior to appear and take them from their day-to-day tribulations. Remember how the people of Israel looked for a political rescue from their Messiah; when He came as He did, He was not received. Instead He was brutalized and murdered.

One of the many lessons to be learned from the exodus out of Egypt, is the opportunities the Egyptians were given to let the people of Israel go. Pharaoh himself observed time after time the warnings from Moses and the consequences from an almighty God. Pharaoh had to witness 10 plagues against him and his people before his hardened heart released the people. In addition to the unnecessary grief he caused his own people, he lost his own son on the last promise. Even then however, his heart hardened once more and he ordered the pursuit of his former slaves only to lose those in pursuit in the Red Sea.

Noah preached for years while building his ark amidst a sea of mockery. Yet none outside his family were found righteous when the rains came. Just as God had promised, the ark Noah constructed rescued him from the onslaught.

God promised Abraham he would father a great nation too numerous to count. Through the prophets, promises were made surrounding Jesus' birth, the nation of Israel, the promised land, and His second coming. Each of these promises included conditions, that, if left unsatisfied would result in judgment.

The returning Christ is depicted as a lion, not a lamb; a victor, not a victim; a judge, not a defendant; a king, not a servant; a God of power, not a babe in a manger. Our God is a God of judgment. Our God is a God who forewarns. Our God is a God of promises. Our God is a God of righteousness.

I believe all too often we expect Him to forgive us even if we reject Him. Some believe His unending mercy will be extended to those who never knew Him. Others believe that after death they will be given an opportunity to select His way or their prior ways. I do not find any Scripture to support any of these preceding views. I believe we have been offered adequate opportunity to understand His Word and to accept His plan for our lives.

Jesus was quick to identify the shortcomings of those who challenged Him. He was especially harsh to hypocrites. A brief scan of Matthew's gospel reveals the following words Jesus offered to get the attention of those who needed it:

- Jesus referred to the Pharisees and Sadducees as a brood of vipers in Matthew 3:7, 12:34, and 23:33. Luke repeats these words in 3:7.

- The parable of the rich fool who lost his life that very night is depicted in Luke 12:20

- Jesus used the word "foolish" to describe those who heard His words but did not put them into practice in Matthew 7:26. Again in Matthew, Jesus described the women in the parable of the ten virgins as foolish in verses 25:2, 25:3, and 25:8

- Jesus issued a stern series of warnings against hypocrites in Matthew 6:2, 6:5, 6:16; 15:7; 16:3; 22:18; 23:13, 23:14, 23:15, 23:23, 23:25, 23:27, 23:29; and 24:51. Chapter 23 includes seven woes to the hypocrites. Similar warnings were captured in Mark 7:6 and Luke 11:44 and 12:56.

- Jesus rebuked hypocritical judgment in Matthew 7:5, Luke 6:42, 12:56, and 13:15.

- Jesus at one point questioned Peter's willingness to understand the events and teachings he had observed when Jesus asked "Are you still so dull?"

- A total of 14 woes is delivered in Matthew; every woe was delivered by Christ himself. The word does not appear in the Gospels unless Jesus uses it; and He used it at least 30 times as He presented warnings.

- Matthew 23:24 describes Christ's use of the phrase "you blind guides"; in 23:17 "you blind fools"; in 23:33 "You snakes! you brood of vipers!"; in 18:17 "treat him as you would a pagan or tax collector"; and in 16:23 "get behind me, Satan" in response to Peter who spoke against Jesus' agenda in the coming days.

- Jesus declared "Go tell that fox, ... " in Luke 13:32. Explaining those who opposed Him, Jesus rebuked in John 8:44: "You belong to your father, the devil, and you want to carry out your father's desire." Jesus continued in 8:55: "Though you do not know him, I know him. If I said I did not, I would be a liar like you, but I do know him and keep his word."

The purpose of the preceding Scriptures is to illustrate that Jesus did not accept the behavior of all those around Him. On the contrary, He directly and sternly responded to those around Him who were outside the will of the Father. The Egyptians suffered the same fate after repeated warnings. Those who lived in the time of Noah received ongoing warnings. We, too, receive warnings. I do not believe we can expect Him to return and heal the sick (although He will put an end to death and sickness); instead He will destroy death. We cannot expect Him to feed the poor; instead He will vanquish poverty. We cannot expect Him to return as a babe; instead He will return as a raging warrior to rescue His people in days that, had He not cut short, would have destroyed all life.

In Genesis heaven and earth were created; at His next coming they will be cleansed. In Genesis the evil one entered; at His next coming the evil one will be eternally bound. In Genesis sin was introduced; at His next coming sin will be contained. In Genesis the death of man entered; at His next coming, death will be repealed. In Genesis sorrow entered man's life; at His second coming sorrow will be replaced with comfort.

## The Value of Fear

The value of fear, the love of fear, the joy of fear; those expressions might sound like the babbling of a crazy person. Which of the following would you pick as a good definition of fear?

a.  an unpleasant, often strong emotion caused by anticipation or awareness of danger

b.  anxious emotion

c.  reason for alarm

d.  profound reverence and awe especially toward God

e.  the way all of us should revere God Almighty!

Answers a. through d. come from Webster's Seventh New Collegiate Dictionary. They provide a good dictionary definition of the word. Answer "e" is the one I felt before checking Webster. Answers "d" and "e" are the uses of the word "fear" that fit the above notions of value, love, and joy. The word "fear" appears about 400 times in the Bible.

While this is not going to be an exhaustive scan of each one, there are some very useful lessons concerning fear.

The first use of fear is in Genesis 9 when God made a covenant with Noah. God put every one of His creatures on the earth at the disposal of mankind. In this first instance, fear was good for man!

> "The fear and dread of you will fall upon all the beasts of the earth and all the birds of the air, upon every creature that moves along the ground, and upon all the fish of the sea; they are given into your hands." (Genesis 9:2)

The second use of the word fear is found in Genesis 15. The NIV translates the word "afraid" rather than "fear." Please note that neither word alters the meaning or intent of the verse. In this second instance, man was comforted by God's presence and promise. A vast number of uses of the word fear in the Bible are followed by the word "not." In these instances, God encourages man in order to receive something He has promised or planned for us.

> "After this, the word of the Lord came to Abram in a vision: 'Do not be afraid, Abram. I am your shield, your very great reward'." (Genesis 15:1)

Skipping a couple hundred occurrences of the word fear (I promised not to examine each one), we come to one of my favorite verses on fear. Many other verses also carry this theme. He who is in God's will needs only fear God for He will conquer every other fear and provide for every other need! In this context, fear is a good and positive emotion to possess. This particular verse is Proverbs 1. Solomon, its author, again was the wisest man ever to live. Solomon presents us with both the positive effects of fear, and the consequences of its absence.

> "The fear of the Lord is the beginning of knowledge, but fools despise wisdom and discipline." (Proverbs 1:7)

Let's fast forward again to Acts 5:11, 9:31, and 10:35. In these verses the reverence of God and His commands are depicted. In the last two of the verses we see the impact of the fear. These also are very positive in working towards the good of God. We begin at a time in the early church when Christians were selling their land and houses and bringing the proceeds into the church. A man named Ananias and his wife Sapphira also sold a piece of land but held back part of the proceeds for themselves. Apparently in an attempt to deceive the apostles they brought forth the offering as if it were complete.  First Ananias came to the apostles that day and upon making his offering, Peter, filled with the knowledge from the Holy Spirit, rebuked him for his deceitfulness. Ananias dropped dead at Peter's feet.  He was wrapped and carried out. About three hours later his wife also came to the apostles.  She told Peter the offering was the full price they paid for the land.  She too dropped dead at Peter's feet and was carried out and buried next to her husband.  The result was

"Great fear seized the whole church and all who heard about these events." (Acts 5:11)

Before moving directly to the other verses in Acts here are a few observations.  One, Sapphira came into the "church" three hours after her husband.  That would be one long service by today's standards.  I realize Catholics aren't the only denomination that "leave the service early" (usually on their way back from communion).   Other denominations leave early during the "invitation."  These services usually last between 45 minutes and 75 minutes.  In the early church, believers were apparently there quite some time.  (You may think they needed church more than we because we are already so much closer to God, having a chance to read the Bible and have history on our compact discs.  Do not be too sure!)  Two, can you imagine going to church and those practicing deceit falling dead on the spot?  I'm not sure more people would attend church or if anyone would be left to attend.

What was the value of the fear that seized the whole church in Acts 5:11?  Acts provides an answer and incorporates the word fear again.

"Then the church throughout Judea, Galilee and Samaria enjoyed a time of peace.  It was strengthened; and encouraged by the Holy Spirit, it grew in number, living in the fear of the Lord." (Acts 9:31)

Peter provides the last of the quotations from Acts.

"Then Peter began to speak: "I now realize how true it is that God does not show favoritism but accepts men from every nation who fear him and do what is right." (Acts 10:34)

In this example God accepts everyone who fears Him; what a great message for Peter to affirm!  How blessed Peter was to be filled with the Holy Spirit.  Thank you, Lord, for Peter!

Thank you, Lord, for also making your Word personal. Paul now describes how we are to grow in the Lord.

> "Therefore, my dear friends, as you have always obeyed–not only in my presence, but now much more in my absence– continue to work out your salvation with fear and trembling, for it is God who works in you to will and to act according to his good purpose." (Philippians 2:12)

No doubt the reverence and respect for the Lord are captured again in this verse. The importance is to remember it applies to each one of us individually. Peter reinforces this particular theme in Peter.

> "Since you call on a Father who judges each man's work impartially, live your lives as strangers here in reverent fear." (1 Peter 1:17)

One could argue that the Old Testament is in the past or the New Testament applies to only some of us today (although I would not agree with either completely). Yet I contend the fear of God makes its way into our futures as well. In the days that are yet to come, the angels proclaim:

> "He said in a loud voice, 'Fear God and give him glory, because the hour of judgment has come ...'" (Revelation 14:7)

I do fear God and I do fear His judgment, but even more I praise Him for His grace, salvation, and His role in my life. These verses end on a note of fear with a quotation from the throne in Heaven found in Revelation.

> "Then a voice came from the throne, saying: 'Praise God, all you his servants, you who fear him, both small and great'!" (Revelation 19:5)

Fear, found in the first book of the Bible. Fear, found in the last book of the Bible. Fear, an emotion God sweeps from us as it pertains to fearing others. Fear, something God instills within us so that we can know Him and His will even better. Fear, the beginning of true knowledge. Fear, the beginning of an eternal relationship with God. Fear, it's not just an irrational emotion about events that may never happen. If I could write songs, I think I'd rewrite the song "I Wish You Love" and name it "I Wish You Fear." Fear, its value, its love, its joy. If it still sounds crazy, I'll just have to accept that.

This flavor of fear is different from some of the fears I once witnessed and experienced: fears of getting my knuckles cracked with a ruler in first grade, fears of having my clothes (not underclothes) removed by a nun in a third grade classroom (yes, this actually did happen as a disciplinary action intended to humiliate one of the boys in the class; no, there did not appear to be any intended "sexual" attack on the part of the nuns), fears of burning in hell for eating the wrong food on the wrong day, fears of eternal damnation for missing a holy day of obligation, fears of separation from God for not supporting the man-made doctrines of the Catholic church. The Bible teaches us to fear God and not man. That's the type of fear I desire.

## What's Wrong With This Picture? (Can You See Through This Window?)

A popular children's television show presents its audience with a series of pictures and then leads the viewer to select the picture that is different from the others. The answer was usually obvious (to me and) even to the intended audience. In much the same way, I felt as if there was something wrong with a picture I was presented at the Catholic Ministries Conference conducted in Albuquerque in the mid 1980s.

The conference was conducted at the local convention center. Hundreds of people attended. I learned about a number of important ministries in the area that were not under the jurisdiction of the Catholic church. A number of curriculum suppliers were available to promote their materials and answer questions about the use of their programs. As a religious education teacher, the church sponsored my registration. I was excited about the things I was learning at the conference.

Similar to other states and regions, New Mexico is rich with a local culture maintained by the Spanish, Native Americans, and more recently a number of other ethnic groups. The Catholic church has been deeply rooted since the early days of Spanish colonization. I did not realize how important the Native American influence was in the local Catholic church until the close of the conference.

That evening, the conference concluded with a service. During the service, a Native American came onto the stage. With incense burning he danced what was described as a ritual dance to one of his gods. While I am not knowledgeable in the worship practices of the Native

American, I do recognize when worship is directed to someone or something other than Jesus Christ. The Catholic church coordinated this "fellowship" which I personally found tragic and embarrassing as a Christian. Of course the Catholic church offered no clarification or apology for the ordeal later. Worse yet, I doubt many of the Catholics who attended either recognized or expressed any horror in having observed, and participated, in what was anything but Christian fellowship. Accepting the non-scriptural practices of the people whose land we share is also exemplified (later in this section) as a Catholic community designed their stained glass windows to imitate the idolatry of the earth elements.

This event planted a seed of doubt in my mind. How could the Catholic church, which claims to be a Christian institution, based on the teachings of the Bible, allow or adopt the local traditions for their own ceremony? The words throughout Deuteronomy, where the Lord reminded His people not to adopt the ways of the people of the lands they would inherit, shook in my heart. Instead, God told the people to tear down the worship poles, altars, and statues in the lands they were to enter. God told them not to spare the people of those lands; nor to take them as slaves nor as wives.

With the Bible as background, how could the events I was experiencing have taken place? Could other traditions also contradict God's Word? Was I within God's will if I did not seek to know Him one-on-one? Other questions surfaced later and intensified as time continued. What kind of father was I to allow my children to grow up in my own ungodly ways? Am I following God as a husband? Do I have responsibilities towards my parents, brother, and two sisters? My comfort level was never the same after that ministries conference.

Not long after that conference I was distraught again; this time during a mass. The priest was taking a few minutes to admire the new stained glass windows that were being installed as part of a refurbishing of the church building. The new windows would be more energy efficient, which seemed reasonable. He went on to describe how the first window in particular, was a reflection of the flood of Noah's time. Had the priest stopped there, he would not have replaced the Word of God with the tradition (and error) of his own knowledge. He went on to say that the flood of Noah's time did not cover the entire earth but was a local flood; clearly deviating from the Biblical account of the flood (see Genesis 7:19 - 20). An event that could have been used to glorify God and witness to His faithfulness was instead used to promote worldly wisdom over Scripture. Many churches may promote their own wisdom but I had witnessed it a number of times exceeding my tolerance level for the treatment of the Word.

Soon thereafter our family began to attend services at a closer and newer parish. They, too, held a very special place in their hearts for their windows. This adoration was reflected in the parish newsletter [3]. The Word of God was not as directly violated, but it was obvious that more attention was being placed on the place of worship rather than the only true and worthy object of worship. The Pastor extracted from Matthew Fox's <u>Creation Spirituality/Liberating Gifts for the Peoples of the Earth</u> by summarizing the four paths of Positiva, Negativa, Creativa, and Transformativa. A part of each of the four "paths" is examined respectively.

1. Positiva

"In the awe, wonder and mystery of nature and of all beings, each of whom is a "word of God", ... "

We all share as being part of God's mighty creation. Once we begin to think that we are also "little gods" we have stepped well beyond Biblical evidence. John magnifies the Word of God at the start of his Gospel.

"In the beginning was the Word, and the Word was with God, and the Word was God. He was with God in the beginning."
(John 1:1)

In addition to reminding us of His omnipresence, John makes clear the Word was God. When we attempt to alter His Word we are attempting to alter God Himself. In order to perpetuate such an effect we would have to be as powerful as God—in essence believing that we are as quoted from Fox "each a word of God." At least a few other religions advocate that doctrine—that they too, will someday be gods. Sorry, but such hopes are not part of the Scripture. John gives us further insight in his first epistle.

"Dear friends, now we are children of God, and what we will be has not yet been made known. But we know that when he appears, we shall be like him, for we shall see him as he is."
(1 John 3:2 - 3)

John clarifies that what we are going to be is not yet known. He says that we shall be like him (not that we will be as He is) and that we will see Him as He is which I contend implies viewing Christ in all His glory. This would be a much more worthy message of inscribing into a series of windows dedicated to the Lord.

2. Negativa

" ... in the silence and emptying, in the letting go and letting be, ... "

The word empty is found five times in the New Testament. Four of its uses describe a person being sent away or left "empty." Each of its uses portrays a negative outcome. The Bible never encourages us to empty ourselves or our spirits. The opposite is true. Repeatedly, we are told to fill ourselves in the Spirit and to walk in the Spirit. At least five times in Acts we are told of the Apostles being filled with the Spirit. In Paul's letters we are told to be filled with the Spirit, fruits of righteousness, knowledge, and joy. James speaks of being filled in peace.

The acts of "emptying" and "letting go" have a lot more to do with eastern mysticism than Biblical teaching. As an example, the Hindus burn their dead to ensure their souls will be released and allowed to go onto their next incarnation. When the Catholic church claims to be the universal church, it's obvious from the canons of Trent, that it does not mean accepting the teachings of the universe; yet to some degree, many forms of non-Christian practices and traditions have found a warm home in the Catholic church.

3. Creativa

"In our generativity we co-create with God"

The book of Genesis is quite certain regarding who the created is and who the Creator is. This message is consistent throughout the New Testament also and is carried through to the last book of the Bible. Here are a few of the references to "created" as found in the New Testament.

"and to make plain to everyone the administration of the mystery, which for ages past was kept hidden in God, who created all things." (Ephesians 3:9)

"For by him all things were created: things in heaven and on earth, visible and invisible, whether thrones or powers or rulers or authorities; all things were created by him and for him." (Colossians 1:16)

"You are worthy, our Lord and God, to receive glory and honor and power, for you created all things, and by your will they were created and have their being." (Revelation 4:11)

"And he swore by him who lives for ever and ever, who created the heavens and all that is in them, the earth and all that is in it, and the sea and all that is in it, and said, 'There will be no more delay'!" (Revelation 10:6)

These verses teach us something in addition to who the Creator is; the Colossians verse specifically teaches us why we were created: "created by him and for him." We were created for Him. We are told to serve Him. As co-creators we now begin to serve ourselves; a simple, tragic, and all too familiar act of selfishness. Let God be glorified in all of our works and let all of our works be done unto His glory only.

4. Transformativa

"The windows also represent the Native American blessing of the four ways, the four directions, the four seasons, the four major elements (earth, water, wind and fire) as well as the concepts of creation spirituality."

The preceding comments on Negativa alluded to the acceptance of non-Scriptural customs into the Catholic church. A couple of paragraphs earlier, the influence of Native Americans in Catholic conferences was shared. The words of acceptance of the Native American culture into the Catholic church are captured again in this church newsletter. I propose another meaning of the "transformativa." Let's celebrate our transformation into the likeness of Christ. Let's applaud the grace He has delivered to accommodate the transformation in our lives. Let's proclaim His transformation away from our sinful nature. I also propose another set of options for the number four. Let the "fours" represent the four books of the Gospel. Let the "fours" remind us of the four horsemen in Revelation. Let the "fours" help us recall the thousands of men in Matthew 15:38. Let all we do bring us gratefully before His throne, recognizing His majesty, and praising His greatness.

During the Easter season of 1992 the Albuquerque Journal printed an article entitled Moving–Heaven and Earth [4].  This story described the stained glass windows in an Episcopal church.  The following three quotations capture the essence of the story

"It provides a magical kind of space that people can be in."

"When it is well done, stained glass can create a sense of "otherness" to a place–a feeling of mystery that adds to the worship experience,   yet, he said, it's not just artistic windows that makes a place sacred."

"A place has a presence about it that has to do with memories and people praying in it, ... Here's a place where I and others have prayed and poured out our souls and have really found unity with other people.  That makes it a holy place."

Words like "magical", "otherness", "sacred", "mystery", "a presence", "holy place", "unity" are used to describe the property, yet not one word about God!  Is it not God's presence that makes a place holy?  When the objects of man's creation become more important than the Creator, tradition impedes the worshippers' intimacy with the Lord.  Avoid any object that may become the recipient of your affection or attention.

## Historically, the Catholic Church Has Taught It is the Only Church

The following extract is from the first Vatican Council.  Each of the eighteen articles from the Council end with an "anathema," a pronounced curse, to all who disagree with its canons.  The teachings of the first Vatican Council build upon the accumulated doctrines of the Catholic church including the Council of Trent.  In the chapter on the Sacraments, John XXIII, is quoted from Vatican II, as endorsing all the teachings from that infamous council in Trent and Vatican I.  One of the most significant doctrines to emerge from Vatican I was the infallibility and irreformability of the pope.  This doctrine precludes the ability to change Papal decrees, which, of course (according to the teachings of the Catholic church), is unnecessary because the pope cannot be wrong when speaking for the church.

"... that the Roman Pontiff, when he speaks ex cathedra, that is, when in discharge of the office of pastor and doctor of all Christians, by virtue of his supreme Apostolic authority, he defines a doctrine regarding faith or morals to be held by the universal Church, by the divine assistance promised to him in blessed Peter, is possessed of that infallibility with which the divine Redeemer willed that his Church should be endowed for defining doctrine regarding faith or morals; and that therefore such definitions of the Roman Pontiff are irreformable of themselves, and not from the consent of the Church. [5], pages 270 - 271

The Council also declared

"Therefore there is no parity between the condition of those who have adhered to the Catholic truth by the heavenly gift of faith, and of those, led by human opinions, follow a false religion;" [5], page 246

These words reflect and continue the mood of Trent some 300 years earlier. Chapter 4 of the proceeds from the council describe how the Catholic tradition is passed within the papacy.

"For the Holy Spirit was not promised to the successors of Peter, that by his revelation they might make known new doctrine; but that by his assistance they might inviolably keep and faithfully expound the revelation or deposit of faith delivered through the Apostles." [5], page 269

If I read this correctly, this statement implies that those who sit upon the "Throne of Peter" are assisted by Peter or Peter's ghost. If indeed the reference is to Peter's assistance (versus that of the Holy Spirit's) then far more serious problems exist than those being addressed here.

Vatican I occurred just a few years after publication of The Papal Syllabus of Errors from Pius IX in 1864. The Pope addresses some of the common heresies of his day by proclaiming in Part 3 - Article 17

"We may entertain at least a well-founded hope for the eternal salvation of all those who are in no manner in the true Church of Christ." [5], page 217

I suspect that there was kindness intended (or extended) to those separated brethren outside the "true Church." I must admit reluctant skepticism today whenever I read of any church that doctrinally believes that it is the "true church." However, remember that Pius IX was writing against the heresies of his day, and, this being one, certainly implies that the contents of the above statement is not true in accordance with the teachings of the Catholic church.

In Article 18 Pius IX addressed another heresy of that day.

> "Protestantism is nothing more than another form of the same true Christian religion, in which it is possible to be equally pleasing to God as in the Catholic church." [5], page 217 - 218

Clearly again, this heresy cannot be true (according to the Catholic church) which implies that those outside the Catholic church are less pleasing to God and that more importantly, Protestants stake no claim in Christianity; that is, the belief in Jesus Christ.

Now if we recall that just five years later, Vatican I convened and the pope was declared infallible and irreformable when speaking on matters of the church, then these and other heresies addressed by Pius IX are eternally a part of the tradition and teaching of the Catholic church. So too then are the endorsements expressed by John XXIII in recognition of the applicability of the Council of Trent.

In the chapter on The Good News from Second Vatican Council (Sounds a Lot Like the Bad News from Earlier Councils), I explore the continuation of Catholic doctrine and teaching despite attempts to remarket the practices of the Catholic church.

In an attempt to close this chapter I am reminded of the phrase (although I do not know who said it, but they were right) "Being born into a religion is the worst reason to belong to a religion." At that time, in practice, I needed to be born into Christ's family, born again; not stillborn into a system.

| Three things you should know after reading this chapter. |
| --- |

✝ Jesus loves you. No tradition can serve as a substitute for the love He has for His children; the love He has for you.

✝ Jesus seeks a relationship with you. Your relationship with Christ comes from your involvement with Him in your day-to-day life. You will not find it buried in traditions that serve as a reminder of that relationship.

✝ Jesus wants you to love your brothers. Share the message of Christ's love for you with others every day. Bring others to realize that a relationship with Him is personal, direct, and always available.

References

[1] The Holy Bible, Authorized King James Version, Holman Bible Publishers, 1985

[2] The New American Bible, Catholic Bible Publishers, 1970

[3] Ark Biczak, "A Message from our Pastor–The Meanings of our Stained Glass Windows," John XXIII Catholic Community Newsletter Vol. 6., No. 3, September, 1991

[4] Janelle Conaway, "Moving–Heaven and Earth," Albuquerque Journal, April 19, 1992

[5] Philip Schaff, Creeds of Christendom: With a History and Critical Notes, Harper & Brothers, Franklin Square, 1896

*"Born once, die twice.*

*Born twice, die once!"*

# Chapter 3

## Peter, Principle or Principal?

> *"And do not call anyone on earth 'father,' for you have one Father, and he is in heaven."* *(Matthew 23:9)*

Matthew 23:9 is just one way to open this chapter. This verse serves as an eye opener; especially if taken literally. Of course the verse can be taken spiritually which renders it even more alarming.

Many books detail a long hideous history of the popes. The Catholic church tends not to dwell heavily on these past events; in part, because of the exaggerated role of the apostle Peter in the Catholic church and the lineage of popes between Peter and the present. Another reason to ignore past papal atrocities is that they undermine the pope's absolute authority and infallibility. Through this chapter you will be equipped to question and understand the origin and perpetuity of the "Throne of Peter." In a scriptural sense you may also feel challenged once again, to choose between the Word of God or the tradition of man.

Even the origin of the word pope causes discomfort. The Scripture verse introducing this chapter reminds us that our true Father is in heaven not here on earth. Reviewing this verse in the context of its local meaning, (its integration test), reveals a warning from Christ: to avoid applying titles to honor ourselves or others. This interpretation is not inconsistent with the "whole" Bible (system test). This concept is directly reinforced in the first commandment. The words "Holy Father" are only found together in John 17:11 as Jesus addresses His Father. All honor is due to God alone. How ironic then that the single word used to address Catholic priests today is 'father.' A high regard for tradition and an apparent lesser regard for Scripture explains this anomaly. This anomaly is but one of many.

The word pope comes from the Latin 'papas.' The Latin word 'papas' means father. Was this term selected as just an innocent coincidence? Consider that the pope is considered to be the Vicar of Christ on earth. To many, both inside and outside Rome this means the pope is Christ on earth. Webster's Seventh New Collegiate Dictionary defines "Vicar of Christ" as "the Roman Catholic Pope." This same lexicon defines "vicar" as "one serving as a substitute or agent." Words for the substitution of Christ cannot be found anywhere in the Bible; nor is the word substitute found in either testament. Rather Jesus told us specifically who would be sent.

> "And I will ask the Father, and he will give you another Counselor to be with you forever—the Spirit of truth. The world cannot accept him because it neither sees him nor knows him. But you know him, for he lives with you and will be in you." (John 14:17 - 17)

The words Jesus spoke are clearly not about a vicar; but rather, about the Holy Spirit. Please note we were promised the Spirit through whom all understanding or revelation would flow, not the pope as the Catholic church professes. Here are some other descriptions Jesus gave us as to whom we should believe, accept, and follow. Quite directly and clearly Jesus tells us.

> "I am the way and the truth and the life. No one comes to the Father except through me.' John 14:6)

John 3 concurs:

> "For God so loved the world that he gave his one and only Son, that whoever believes in him shall not perish but have eternal life." (John 3:16)

First Corinthians goes on:

> "Now I want you to realize that the head of every man is Christ, ..." (1 Corinthians 11:3)

Finally, Ephesians extols:

> "Christ is the head of the church, his body of which he is the Savior." (Ephesians 5:23)

Please note that this theme is consistent throughout the Bible, both testaments. Also note that not only does this theme apply to studying the role of the pope, but it also applies to every other entity interceding between man and God for salvation.

Jesus did promise to send another to complete our knowledge and understanding as He instructed:

> "Do not leave Jerusalem, but wait for the gift my Father promised, which you have heard me speak about. For John baptized with water, but in a few days you will be baptized with the Holy Spirit." (Acts 1:4 - 5)

Jesus continued in verse 8

> "But you will receive power when the Holy Spirit comes on you; and you will be my witnesses in Jerusalem, and in all Judea and Samaria, and to the ends of the earth." (Acts 1:8)

As soon as He finished He was taken up into the sky until the clouds hid Him. Acts 2 describes the events 10 days later when the Holy Spirit came upon them. Clearly, Jesus did not send an office, a church, or any lineage to fulfill His promises.

## Peter–Legacy, Residency, or Supremacy?

The scriptural account of the apostle Peter is one of the great character studies of the New Testament. Peter was personally called by Christ. Peter had the courage to leave the boat in the storm and begin his walk on water at the call of Christ. Peter jumped to Jesus' rescue, at least in thought and word, when he retorted that he would not let harm come to Jesus after Peter's confession of who Jesus was. Peter was given a new name, as was Abraham from whose seed all men would be blessed. Peter was the apostle who proclaimed the "good news" to the gentiles at Pentecost. Peter performed miracles as recorded in the book of Acts and liars dropped dead at his feet. Yet the Peter of the Bible, a personal companion of the Christ on earth, is not the Peter of the church of Rome; rather, he has become the replacement of Christ throughout the earth in accordance with papal decree.

While some readers may be startled by the next several paragraphs, please review church and secular history regarding the office of the pope.

1.  Peter was not the first pope.  The first pope is recognized as Boniface III who came to power in 610!  Peter's death in 67 or 68 AD preceded the use of this title by more than 500 years.  The title of pope has also been traced to one of Boniface's predecessors, Gregory I the Great, perhaps twenty years earlier, at some point during his reign but not for certain at its beginning.

2.  History contradicts Peter's papacy in Rome.

    •  In a letter from the apostle Paul in approximately 58 AD, wherein he greeted many of the brethren by name and households as well, he did not include Peter's name.  Paul had a habit of mentioning those who turned from him or the faith.  I conclude Paul did not mention Peter's name because Peter was not in Rome.  Certainly Paul would not have overlooked the "bishop of Rome" had such an office existed.

    •  Eusebius, recognized as the father of church history (although I am not calling him father; I am merely restating his assigned title in the church), writes that Peter preached in a number of places (other than Rome) and while delayed in Rome was crucified. He did not describe Peter as bishop of Rome in any of his writings.

    •  According to some accounts, history does not confirm Peter in any way took charge of church communities in Rome.

    •  The early "bishops of Rome" did not include Peter's name in the first lists of the bishops.  Irenaeus, prior to 200 AD documented the first twelve bishops of Rome and began with Linus.  The Apostolic Constitution, as late as 270 AD, also listed Linus as the first bishop of Rome.

Because the word "pope" did not appear until hundreds of years after Peter's death, because history casts a great shadow of doubt upon

Peter's residency (let alone supremacy) in Rome, and because the early church historians make no mention of Peter as the bishop of Rome, I (not to imply that you should) conclude Peter was not the first pope.

Does it really matter whether or not Peter was the first pope? If you possess a personal relationship with the Savior, I would contend "no!" I would contend "yes" if you have placed your faith in the traditions of man, in the acceptance of man's truth over God's Word–a Word that does not lie.

3. Peter did not claim to be pope. What then is the importance of Peter to the Catholic church? Why not accept that Linus was the first bishop of Rome and somebody else was the first pope? The Catholic church has taught another doctrine that is tied directly to Peter from whom the pope and church claim their authority. This controversy begins in Matthew 16:18 but it continues into what can be misinterpreted as Peter's exclusive ordination for administering the kingdom. Because of the importance of Matthew 16:18, I have provided its translation in a number of different Bible versions (all bolding mine).

New American Bible (Catholic authorized version)

"I for my part declare to you, you are '**Rock**', and on this **rock** I will build my church ..."

New International Version

"And I tell you that you are Peter, and on this **rock** I will build my church ..."

King James Version

"And I say unto thee, that thou art Peter, and upon this **rock** I will build my church ..."

Gideon's

"I also tell you that you are Peter, and on this **rock** I will build my church ..."

Life Application Bible

"You are Peter, a stone; and upon this **rock** I will build my church ..."

## A Simple Model For Scriptural Interpretation

We can use a paradigm from the software engineering profession to offer an approach to Biblical interpretation or hermeneutics. A testing model, and I underscore the key word "A", for new software endorses various testing approaches: unit, integration, system, and acceptance. These testing levels can be applied to Scripture as follows:

Unit testing usually includes the test of a module or program by itself and can be compared to the examination of a single verse of Scripture by itself. What does it say that God would want me (us) to know? What does the verse mean and how do I use it to draw nearer to Christ?

Integration testing typically includes testing a program with those programs that directly precede or are directly prerequisite to the successful execution of a program as well as those programs that directly follow or are directly dependent upon the subject program. An analogy in Scripture is the study of the verses that directly precede and follow a verse. This second test ensures that a verse is not taken out of context. Certainly rape, murder, incest, and adultery are found in verses in Scripture; but, none of these activities can be interpreted as God's will if the verses are enclosed with the verses that surround them. In Paul's first letter to the Thessalonians we are all encouraged to test everything, holding onto the good and avoiding all evil (1 Thessalonians 5:21 - 22).

System testing is a complete test of all the programs included in all the cycles associated with a system. In this respect, the parallel in Scripture is to examine all the verses, in context, which are related to a concept. Understanding the Old Testament and the New Testament principles allows us to "take captive every thought to make it obedient to Christ" as recommended in 2 Corinthians 10:5.

Acceptance testing facilitates the verification of cosmetic, convenience, and functional features of the software product as they comply with the expectations of the client. Scripturally, we need to accept God's Word. He's already passed all the tests and He's already accepted us; imperfect as we are. The Bereans were cited for their rigorous searching of the Scriptures daily to test what they heard for its truth.

Having described a model for a more rigorous examination of the Word I must offer a final caveat. I doubt that man can devise a complete and perfect model for understanding something that is already complete and perfect. In other words, if the test was to fail to yield the desired result of knowing our God and growing closer to Him, then it is the test that is necessarily flawed and not the subject of the test–in this instance, the Word of God.

John reminds us in his first epistle not to believe every spirit but to test the spirits to authenticate that is from God. John's advice seems practical in dealing with matters beyond those we perceive to be of the spiritual realm–that is to test the spirit of those from whom we seek daily consultation.

The meaning of this verse, by itself, seems quite clear, that is, until applying the proposed model for scriptural interpretation wherein closer examination provides another meaning.

Test 1 - what do the words mean? Although I have confessed a scarcity of knowledge in Greek I do not believe that relieves me from understanding any Greek nor showing an interest in the original Greek writings. Two different words are used in this verse to describe the words bolded in the above versions of Matthew 16:18. One word is petros. This word is translated into the first bolded set of words above. It means a little stone; the type you might pick up and skim across a lake. The second word is petra. This word is translated into the second bolded set of words above. It means a large heavy stone that a single man cannot move, such as a cornerstone or foundation stone. Its gender is different from petros. The words do not connote the same meaning. The Catholic version, the NAB, subscribes to the difference by using 'Rock' and 'rock'. This difference leads into the second test of the verse.

Test 2 - how do the words fit with the surrounding Scripture? This test shines a clarifying light on the subject and Peter's response. "Response" is the key word for Peter was answering a question. The question had nothing to do with Peter and everything to do with Christ. In Matthew 16:13, Jesus posed the question "Who do people say the Son of Man is?". After responding as to what the crowds of the day were saying Jesus followed up with a more direct question: "But what about you?" .... "Who do you say that I am?". Peter is recorded as having spoken quickly "You are the Christ, the Son of the living God."

From this overview we learn Jesus is teaching the apostles who He is. Peter was rewarded for his prompt and correct response. Remember Jesus did not ask the question "who are you Peter" but "Who do you say that I am?", and Peter's response was to who Jesus was and not who he (Peter) might someday be thought to be. It begins to become clear that when Christ said "upon this rock I will build my church" He was referring to Peter's foundational confession and not Peter the skimming stone. Can this conclusion be confirmed by testing its interpretation with all Scripture, the third or "system" test?

Test 3 - how do the words fit with the rest of Scripture? I will present what I believe to be the most compelling and conclusive evidence first. Peter tells us:

> "As you come to him, the living Stone—rejected by men but chosen by God and precious to him—you also, like living stones, are being built into a spiritual house to be a holy priesthood, offering spiritual sacrifices acceptable to God through Jesus Christ." (1 Peter 2:4)

Peter himself depicts Christ as the living Stone; for Peter had not yet been rejected by men and he therefore could not have been exalting himself. This verse is consistent with Peter's treatment in other Scripture verses. Peter continues on to describe a fulfilled prophecy about the stone laid in Zion and how trusting Him will never lead to shame. Peter continues at some length to talk about the God with whom he physically walked.

> "... Christ suffered for you, leaving you an example, that you should follow in his steps. 'He committed no sin, and no deceit was found in his mouth.'" (1 Peter 2:21 - 22)

Much earlier we saw that this prophecy was one of many Christ fulfilled. From this evidence I believe I can conclude without reservation that Christ alone is the rock of our salvation.

> "He alone is my rock and my salvation" (Psalm 62:2)

> "My salvation and my honor depend on God; he is mighty rock, my refuge: (Psalm 62:6)

> "... for they drank from the spiritual rock that accompanied them, and that rock was Christ." (Psalm 62:7)

The preceding verses are but a few of many verses that confirm from the Old to the New Testament that Christ is the Rock. How right Peter was when he declared "You are the Christ". What a marvelous confession on which to base the foundation of the church!

Paul, too, metaphorically distinguishes between the apostles (not just Peter), the prophets, and Christ.

> "Consequently, you are no longer foreigners and aliens, but fellow citizens with God's people and members of God's household, built on the foundation of the apostles and prophets, with Christ Jesus himself as the chief cornerstone. In him the whole building is joined together and rises to become a holy temple in the Lord." (Ephesians 2:19 - 21)

Is that foundation a faith in Peter or is that foundation a faith in Christ? How could any verse be interpreted to exalt man above God? How could man place his customs and traditions above the will and Word of God? How can we substitute a mere man for an incomparable God? More importantly, does the establishment of Peter or anyone else as pope, and does the tradition-based authority that comes from that office turn our attention to Christ or away from Christ? As for the papacy, as the Vicar (substitution) of Christ on earth, I suspect the latter. Does a belief in the power from Rome break the first commandment by directing our spiritual attention elsewhere? The Byzantine Catholics raise another interesting question: "Were there not 12 apostles, have we forgotten the teachings of the other 11?" (My interpretation of their question targets the "other 11" to include Matthias not Judas.)

The church of Rome traces its genealogy all the way back to Peter as the first pope. Paul told Timothy not to get "mixed up" with endless genealogies.

> "As I urged you when I went into Macedonia, stay there in Ephesus so that you may command certain men not to teach false doctrines any longer nor to devotes themselves to myths and endless genealogies. These promote controversies rather than God's work—which is by faith." (1 Timothy 1:3 - 4)

I think Paul was telling us that genealogies were no longer important. I believe that the perfect bloodline is through the cross and not through the bloodlines of tradition (as they promote arguments). By the bloodline of the cross I mean His atoning sacrifice for us on the cross.

*The perfect bloodline is through the cross—not tradition!*

## Well Then, What About the Other Popes?

This section summarizes some of the acts of the popes, acting on behalf of Christ on earth.  During some papal reigns, history records difficulty in ascertaining who was pope from time to time.  Some popes had very short reigns, at other times it appeared that more than one pope reigned (although not necessarily in Rome), and still other times the pope was not seen or was unavailable and therefore his power could not be confirmed.  I think you will understand some of these stereotypes as you review the abridged list that follows.  For additional detail on these incidents, please refer to Peter De Rosa's <u>Vicars of Christ</u> [1] (indicated by a [1]) from which part of the following list is extracted and many of the papal improprieties following this list are found.  Most of the following references are summarized from <u>Halley's Bible Handbook</u> [2] (indicated by a [2]).  The list is presented in chronological order and is by no means a complete list of papal history.  A final reference, with a slant towards Catholicism but still recording the atrocities of some of the popes, is Jerrold Packard's <u>Peter's Kingdom</u> [3].  Packard describes how John II actually changed his name from Mercury, a Roman pagan god and how Pius III did not become an ordained priest until he was elected pope.

| Pope | Year | Event(s) |
|---|---|---|
| [2]Sergius III | 904 | His mistress Marozia, her mother Theodora, and her sister filled the papal chairs with illegitimate sons and started the 60-year "Rule of Harlots". |
| [1]Stephen VIII | 928 | his ears and nose were cutoff |
| [2]John XI | 931 | was one of Marozia's illegitimate sons |
| [1]Benedict V | 964 | left the country for Constantinople after dishonoring a young girl |
| [1,2]John XII | 955 | assumed papacy at 16, monasteries prayed for his death, slept with his mother, ran a harem in the Lateran Palace, gambled with pilgrim's offerings, gave golden chalices from St. Peter's to his female escorts of the night, toasted devil in front of church's altar, abandoned papacy in fear for life, formally charged with: ordaining a |

| [1,2]John XII (continued) | 955 | deacon in a stable, charging for ordinations copulating with several women, his niece and two sisters invoking demons had over 100 Franciscans burned for believing that Jesus lived in poverty, was killed in the act adultery by an enraged husband |
|---|---|---|
| [2]Boniface VII | 984 | murdered John XIV |
| [1]Benedict VIII | 1012 | bought the "Office of Pope" with bribe money |
| [2]John XIX | 1024 | bought papacy, passed all needed clerical degrees in one day |
| [2]Benedict IX | 1033 | became pope at age 12, murdered and adulterated in daylight, robbed pilgrims on the graves of martyrs, driven from Rome by its residents |
| [2]Gregory VI | 1045 | bought papacy |
| [2]Pius II | 1458 | seduced young women and encouraged young men to seduce young women, reportedly fathered many illegitimate children |
| [2]Paul II | 1464 | filled his house with concubines |
| [2]Sixtus IV | 1471 | decreed that money would deliver souls from Purgatory |
| [2]Innocent VIII | 1484 | had 16 children, various wives, multiplied and sold church offices selling them for vast sums of money for one-twentieth of a Rhenish guilder, Germans could eat milk foods on fast days for a year |
| [2]Alexander VI | 1492 | bought papacy fathered a number of illegitimate children established new cardinals for money his mistress' brother, a cardinal became next pope |
| [2]Leo X | 1513 | excommunicated Martin Luther, appointed a cardinal who was seven years old |
| [2]Clement XI | 1700 | condemned reading of Bible by laity |
| [2]Clement XIV | 1769 | suppressed Jesuits |
| [2]Pius VII | 1800 | restored Jesuits |
| [2]Pius IX | 1854 | Vatican Council (I) which decreed papal infallibility and irreformability |

I want to stop here and examine the last three entries above. When Pius IX decreed infallibility and irreformability, did he not consider the inconsistencies of the papacy's past of which the Jesuit issue is one of many examples? Did Pius not consider the possibility of reform in the future such as happened at Vatican II when eating meat of Fridays became "legal?" What part of God's plan was considered? Did God make any man infallible regardless of his office or position? Does Romans not remind us:

"for all have sinned and fall short of the glory of God," (Romans 6:23)

Does not James also remind us that:

"We all stumble in many ways ...?" (James 3:2)

I know that this includes me and I am reminded daily how imperfect I am. I know that in the past I have stumbled many times.

As blessed as Peter was, Peter too stumbled from time to time. How is it then that mere mortal man has become perfect or made himself to be the perfect substitute? Is it in his own sight or His own sight? We tend to stumble far more when we slip out from the Word and into man-made tradition. Proverbs warns us about our self-reliance.

"Trust in the Lord with all your heart and lean not on your own understanding; in all your ways acknowledge him, and he will make your paths straight. Do not be wise in your own eyes; fear the Lord and shun evil." (Proverbs 3:5 - 7)

"There is a way that seems right to a man but in the end it leads to death." (Proverbs 14:12)

Given the flavor of the aforementioned papal history some very serious questions must be addressed:

First, would Peter have had anything to do with passing on the teachings of Christ with men such as these. I am not proposing that popes or anyone must be without sin—that's not possible. Rather, were these men worthy of representing Christ on earth, how about any church, how about what the Catholic church still considers the only true church?

Second, could they possibly have been a substitution for Christ through whom salvation passes?

Third, if church history had recorded all the facts incorrectly, and in fact Peter was the first pope, would the line of succession be valid any longer? Please reread First Timothy.

"As I urged you when I went into Macedonia, stay there in Ephesus so that you may command certain men not to teach false doctrines any longer nor to devote themselves to myths and endless genealogies. These promote controversies rather than God's work–which is by faith." (1 Timothy 1:3 - 4)

Fourth, could the message of the church, the Word and its original teachings, have survived through the hands of these sins?

I look to and thank those who suffered at the hands of the church to see that the Scriptures survived, were translated into the language of the people, and were entrusted outside the Catholic church for its mere existence.

## A Brief Examination of Indulgences and Purgatory

In order to raise funds for the papacy, a mastermind of finances, John XXII, conceived the sale of forgiveness–more commonly known as indulgences. The faithful could procure their way out of sin and receive absolution for sins like murder and sexual promiscuity. Through this opportunity, the more members sinned, potentially the richer the Catholic church became. Naturally then, more "laws" would lead to more disobediences, and more disobediences to increased papal cash flow. The Roman Chancery went as far as to publish a sin-price catalog. Of course different folks paid different prices. As an example, a deacon could be released of murder for 20 crowns, a bishop or abbot forgiven of assassination for 300 livres. German laity were allowed to pay for a year-long right, in advance of course, to eat certain foods typically avoided on days of fasting.

Unsatisfied by the greed of selling to the living, this new fund raiser was also applied to those still in purgatory. Purgatory had been concocted hundreds of years earlier and surely must have accumulated lots of souls since that time. Now church members could help buy their departed loved ones out of this "limbo" state. A Dominican named Tetzel literally marketed indulgences in Germany using phrases like:

[1] "As soon as the coin in the coffers rings,   A soul from Purgatory springs.";

[1] Declaring that twelve pence would enable a son to win his father's release from agony; and

[2] "As soon as your coin clinks in the chest the souls of your friends will rise out of Purgatory into Heaven."

Unfortunately, this practice continues today as masses are said for the dead.   Catholic church workers testify that the church still maintains separate accounts for receipts from masses to release souls from purgatory.   Others have called purgatory the best fund raiser ever devised in the Catholic church.

On page 56 of the definition section in the back of the New American Bible [4] includes Purgatory.   That definition is dissected and reviewed in the following eight quotations.

> 1.   "That place or state of punishment where the souls of those who have died in the state of grace, ... "

Still unsure if purgatory should be a place or a state, it is asserted as a punishment.   This assertion implies that our Father has further punishment in store for us after we pass from this life.   Aside from not finding this particularly appealing, I cannot find it anywhere in the Bible.   The 'tradition' of purgatory, adopted around 600 AD, must have also left a number of souls in this limbo state that passed from earthly life prior to that time.

> 2.   "... but who still may have some unrepented venial sins or may have to make satisfaction for forgiven mortal sins, suffer until admitted into heaven."

We should realize by now that we cannot make "satisfaction" for our own sins.   Christ did that for us almost 2000 years ago.   When Christ died upon the cross He said "It is finished" the actual Greek words were the same "Paid in full" that canceled legal debt during His time.   Our acceptance of Christ as our personal savior releases us from the debt of the sin we had acquired to that point and sin that we will commit after that point.   When He bore our sins on the cross it was for the "sin of man", committed and yet to be committed.   Unfortunately Scripture differs; you cannot save yourself; you can accept His atonement and spend eternity with Him or without Him.

3. "The Church proves the Doctrine of Purgatory."

The definition does not describe how the Catholic church proves the existence of purgatory; although, this would seem to be an excellent place to offer such an explanation.

4. "Sacred Scripture in the Old Testament, relates how Judas Maccabeus sent 12,000 drachmas of silver to Jerusalem for sacrifice to be offered for the sins of the dead."

The act of Judas Maccabeus is not something Jesus ever endorsed nor taught. A more interesting question is why the books of Maccabeus are included in the Catholic version of the Bible. The author of this book acknowledges that he is not a prophet in 1 Maccabees 9:27. Maccabees is considered one of the Apocrypha books and along with others is not considered inspired by most denominations. More suspect from a credibility standpoint for Catholics is why these books were not accepted by the Catholic church until the infamous Council of Trent, in the sixteenth century. Even early church founders like Jerome, who wrote the Latin Vulgate, which was the Bible of the Catholic church for centuries, strongly protested the inclusion of this book in the Holy Scriptures. Jesus paid to Caesar what was Caesar's but never offered currency to the Father for salvation for Himself or anyone else.

5. "Through the inspiration of the Holy Spirit, the writer of the book wrote, 'It is therefore a holy and a wholesome thought to pray for the dead that they may be loosed from their sins.' Christ Himself inferred there are sins which can be forgiven after death: 'Whoever says anything against the Holy Spirit will not be forgiven, either in this age or in the age to come.' That complete satisfaction must be made is noted by Christ, 'I warn you, you will not be released until you have paid the last penny.'"

As presented above, these passages are offered as if they appear together in Matthew 12:32. Please look for yourself and see if these verses are presented together; they are not. Perhaps the authors of the dictionary that accompanies the New American Bible did not expect anyone to review these definitions or did expect the reader to believe without looking. Please explore the Word for yourself!

6. "Holy Scripture also tells us that "there shall not enter anything defiled" into heaven. Therefore, it is logical to reason that a soul in the state of grace but with venial sin

staining it must be cleansed of the venial sin before
entering heaven."

The commentary (associated with the second quotation) is equally
applicable to the preceding quotation. The bracketed clarification in
the next quotation is the author's.

7.  "In Purgatory the poor souls primarily suffer a pain of loss,
    because, while there, they cannot see the Beatific
    Vision." [being face-to-face with Christ]

Was it a slip of the pen when the adjective "poor" was selected to
describe the souls in purgatory in conjunction with seeing God face-to-
face? Earlier phrases within this definition certainly allude to the
notion of payment for sins. How do the poor pass from purgatory? How
do the sin-stained who have poor relatives pass from purgatory? How
do those who have no family or friends pass from purgatory with no one
knowing of them? Who judges those who go to Purgatory? Who
releases souls from purgatory and either serving time or having been
paid out by other earthly intercessors? How do we resolve tradition
when it is not supported by Scripture?

8.  "The realization that their sins alone prevent this
    happiness causes dreadful suffering. Too, knowing that
    the soul did not take advantage of any opportunities of
    purging it of sin while still living adds to the torture."

If this soul is "not living" how can it suffer in torture? Does this really
sound like God's plan for us after we pass from this earth? Compare this
logic with the apostle John's.

"He who has the Son has life; he who does not have the Son of
God does not have life." (1 John 5:12)

John does not describe a third alternative, nor does Scripture; only
tradition can maintain the concept of purgatory. Jesus made it so
simple, why does man have to add to and muddy God's simple plan?
Ask God to unfold His plan in your life. Please do not hesitate, seek
Him now. Ask Him into your life. Confess to Him your sins. Accept
His Son's sole atonement for your sins. Use His Word to strengthen your
relationship with Him daily. Talk to Him. He's there—a mere syllable
away—LORD!

Paul spoke about death, and more than once.  In Philippians Paul ignores the possibility of Purgatory as a consequence of death.

> "For to me, to live is Christ and to die is gain.  If I am to go on living in the body, this will mean fruitful labor for me.  Yet what shall I choose?  I do not know!  I am torn between the two:  I desire to depart and be with Christ, which is better by far;"  (Philippians 1:21 - 23)

Is it possible that one on the writers of the Bible did not himself know about this contrived God's plan for self-redemption?  Since Paul was inspired by the Holy Spirit (remembering that the Spirit is truth) is it likely that Paul was misguided in his claims or merely allowed to write outside the authority of God Himself?  Could Paul have erred twice in his thinking?  In his second letter to the Corinthians, he expressed death this way:

> "We are confident, I say, and would prefer to be away from the body and at home with the Lord."  (2 Corinthians 5:8)

In this verse Paul reassures us that believers are not at home in the flesh, but rather we are at home when we leave our fleshy bodies and reside with Christ.  In much the same way Paul reminded us in Philippians 3:20 that our citizenship is in heaven.  I find no room for contradiction in Paul's teaching, but I find unresolved conundrums in accommodating Purgatory with these teachings.  David must also have been unaware of the existence of Purgatory.  In Psalm he writes

> "Precious in the sight of the Lord is the death of his saints."  (Psalm 116:15)

Once again, the conspicuous absence of Purgatory is evident.  I believe our deaths are precious because of the joy God shares in being reunited with his children—a reunion that lasts for eternity.  I thank you Lord that You have taught us repeatedly and consistently throughout the Word, that we rely solely on You Lord for salvation and atonement.

Today, the Vatican continues to solicit funds to support itself; now applying technological innovation.  A brief article was recently printed that promoted a new papal fund raiser—"Dial-A-Pope."  [5]  For a mere $1.95 a minute, you can hear a taped message from John Paul II.  The messages are two to three minutes in length equating to almost a $6.00 phone call.  Not to ignore a large potential pool of callers, a special number has been established in Spanish.  Proceeds are expected to help reduce the large Vatican deficit.

No mention is made in the article concerning efforts to improve papal fiscal management.    The article included no benefit to the caller although I suspect that the intended benefit is to hear from the pope.  I would recommend that folks save their money and open their Bibles. The message can't be topped and it's a lot less costly.

In an article published a year earlier entitled "The Vatican suffers financial woes," [6] the archbishop of Santa Fe seeks additional donations to the PETER'S PENCE fund.    The article includes the following points.

•    It lists the prior year's Vatican operating deficit at roughly 86 million dollars.  It does not offer the total amount of the operating budget.

•    It refers to the Catholic church as the "Universal Church."  I suspect that a "universal church" provides a wider appeal to the entire "Christian community" especially appropriate during fund raising efforts.

•    It describes other services and institutions such as a medical staff, local bank, post office, radio station, daily newspaper, attorneys, and museum; it does not identify how many of the poor are clothed, the destitute sheltered, the hungry feed, or the lost saved.

•    It repeatedly refers to the pope as the "Holy Father." It refers to the pope as the "Vicar of Christ" and the "successor of Peter."

I believe that organizations established to support the Lord's work are accountable for sound fiscal administration as well as being responsible for the funds in which they are entrusted.  The apostle Paul made tents so as to avoid being a financial burden to his hosts while he preached. Christ developed His followers; the papacy appears to be developing land.  The descriptions of the pope serve to validate that the pope's role is as sensationalized today as it has ever been.  The papacy itself has entered into a new era of indulgence–self-indulgence.

## Why Escape from Purgatory?

"Escape from Purgatory" offers an alternative to a well-known tradition retaining Catholic church members in bondage.  They cannot leave the church; they are taught salvation comes only through the Catholic church and its traditions. Historically they have been discouraged from reading the Bible. It was a sin to have the Bible in the language of the people. The Catholic church burned those who translated the Bible into common language. It was a mortal sin to read a "Protestant" Bible or attend a "Protestant" service. How was anyone to learn what God's plan was? God's Word was replaced by tradition (officially tradition was placed on par with Scripture during the Council of Trent) and Catholic church members were not allowed to read the Bible in their native language. Catholic church members were taught that they were not equipped to read and understand Scripture by themselves. You will find these same behavioral patterns in cults. For a more detailed look at cults refer to Breese's "Know the Mark of Cults".

The connotation of the word "purgatory" exemplifies the entire breadth of the mistruths of tradition in the Catholic church. Many of these traditions come directly from pagan religions as the church grew. Hundreds of years passed before praying to saints was accepted, the notion of purgatory arose, or the term "pope" was adopted. These are the traditions we must leave behind; clinging instead to Christ, His atonement, and His Word. Paul said it best in his second letter to the Corinthians.

"We demolish arguments and every pretension that sets itself
up against the knowledge of God and we take captive every
thought to make it obedient to Christ." (2 Corinthians 10:5)

Our knowledge of God comes through a personal relationship with Him, reading His Word, and accepting His plan. Each of these aspects of our relationship with Him comes through His Son, Jesus Christ and through no other man, alive or deceased, laity or church official, group or ritual.

Purgatory is but one of the Catholic church's teachings that I had a difficult time reconciling as I began to read through the Bible. Purgatory is the notion that initially caused me to doubt the integrity of the Catholic church. What does the Bible say about death and judgment? Hebrews states that

"Just as man is destined to die once, and after that to face
judgment," (Hebrews 9:27)

Please note that there is no intercession, no intermission, nor any intervention between death and judgment. As believers in Christ, no other action beyond death precedes our time with the Father.

The Old Testament also makes clear.

> "No man can redeem the life of another or give to God a ransom for himself." (Psalm 49:7)

Because this truth is revealed about our physical life, and because there exists no evidence to the contrary about our spiritual life in the Bible, I reasonably believe that we can and should apply this concept to that everlasting life of which we can be assured beyond this life.

I believe that there are three key events in a persons' life; when they are born, and when they die. Because I believe in the significance of three events, one of the events must occur twice. Perhaps a slogan best represents how we alone are responsible for deciding to follow Christ's teachings. I am unaware of the original source of the following words, but their value is timeless (at least until His second coming.)

> "Born once, die twice.
>
> Born twice, die once!"

John explains Jesus' reason for our second birth.

> "In reply Jesus declared, 'I tell you the truth, no one can see the kingdom of God unless he is born again'." (John 3:3)

Revelation describes the innocuous second death of the believer.

> "He who has an ear, let him hear what the Spirit says to the churches. He who overcomes will not be hurt at all by the second death." (Revelation 2:11)

Revelation 20 restates the same principle. Scripture describes that God already has the plan for our forgiveness.

> "That God was reconciling the world to himself not counting men's sins against them. And he has committed to us the message of reconciliation. We are therefore Christ's ambassadors, as though God were making his appeal through us. We implore you on Christ's behalf: Be reconciled to God." (Revelation 20:6)

This phrase is found in 2 Corinthians 5:19 - 20. This reconciliation is to God and through God. Because He is not counting our sins, no intercession of prayers or offerings can reconcile us further once saved.

Often I'm asked why, if I believe in a God of infinite mercy, love, and forgiveness, that I do not also believe that God would allow a soul to be saved after death. Ever since Eve stumbled in the Garden, man has continued to assert his plan as the better plan before God. God is also omniscient—all knowing. Therefore, man cannot possibly have a better plan than God. If man considers himself more wise than God, than perhaps one could reason that God is wrong in the judgments that He has also promised for ignoring Him and His Word. Satan had another plan, too, and I believe he wins when man thinks he's going to be in a position to barter at death. I think Satan wins when man ignores God's plan for salvation and man rests on the assurance that those he leaves behind can labor him into heaven.

Peter also reminded us in his second epistle 2:1 - 3

"But there were also false prophets among the people, just as there will be false teachers among you. They will secretly introduce destructive heresies, even denying the sovereign Lord who bought them—bringing swift destruction on themselves. Many will follow their shameful ways and will bring the way of truth into disrepute. In their greed these teachers will exploit you with stories they have made up. Their condemnation has long been hanging over them, and their destruction has not been sleeping." (2 Peter 2:1 - 3)

Purgatory challenges the integrity of the Catholic church's teachings and doctrines. Purgatory challenges man's traditions. Purgatory is an open and closed case Scripturally speaking. If you open the Word, you will not find it. Case closed!

## Celibacy—God's Plan or Man's?

Approximately 1000 years after Peter's death, another new tradition was introduced to the Catholic church. I hope that the word "tradition" begins to raise instant suspicion at its mere mention. I believe that this suspicion is what John meant when he wrote:

"See that what you have heard from the beginning remains in you. If it does, you also will remain in the Son and in the Father." (1 John 2:4)

What has happened to the early church teachings? What has happened to teaching from the Word of God rather than the tradition of man? New traditions continue to infiltrate the body of Christ though, even today.

This new tradition was celibacy. Five hundred years later, at the Council of Trent it was described as a state of perfection. Ironically, many Catholics were already living in what was called "Holy Matrimony," by then a recognized sacrament according to the Catholic church. So what we have is an imperfect state for the laity–Holy Matrimony, and a perfected state for the priesthood–celibacy; both of which the Catholic church describes as God-sent sacraments. Celibacy brought new problems of hypocrisy to the Catholic church. Two examples of those early problems are extracted from Vicars of Christ pages 118, 120, 120, and 141 respectively.

- Cardinal Hugo, wrote to the population of Lyons in the name of the pope in 1250 with thanks: "During our residence in your city, we have been of very charitable assistance to you. On our arrival, we found scarcely three or four purchasable sisters of love, whilst at our departure we leave you, so to say, one brothel that extends from the western to the eastern gate."

- Women began taken daggers with them to confession–fearing the celibates on the other side of the confessional.

- The reason for so many prostitutes in Rome–so many celibates.

- Savonarola, a Florentine friar described the nuns as worse than harlots.

Earlier examples, both prior to and after the proclamation of the doctrine of celibacy, suggest widespread papal indiscretions. Despite the "perfected state" of celibacy proclaimed by the Catholic church at Trent, we need to recognize that Peter was not celibate. Anyone who suggests such a lifestyle would have a difficult time explaining Matthew 8:14 when Jesus healed Peter's mother-in-law. This teaching of the Catholic church remains a controversy with other orthodox churches as well that never accepted this doctrine of the Catholic church almost 1000 years ago.

Paul wrote Timothy about this very matter. First, Paul presented the qualifications of overseers and deacons.

> "Now the overseer must be above reproach, the husband of but one wife, temperate, self-controlled, respectable, hospitable, able to teach, ..." (1 Timothy 3:2)

> "... In the same way, their wives are to be women worthy of respect, not malicious talkers but temperate and trustworthy in everything. A deacon must be the husband of but one wife and must manage his children and his household well."
> (1 Timothy 3:11 - 12)

Paul uses the same words for describing elders in the church in Titus 1:6. From Paul's words, clearly men who served as officials in the church were allowed to be married and that a test of their abilities was the management of their own households. But Paul goes further to issue a stern warning in his letter to Timothy:

> "The Spirit clearly says that in later times some will abandon the faith and follow deceiving spirits and things taught by demons. Such teachings come through hypocritical liars, whose consciences have been seared as with a hot iron. They forbid people to marry and order them to abstain from certain foods which God created to be received with thanksgiving by those who believe and who know the truth."
> (1 Timothy 4:1 - 3)

Verses do exist in the Bible that encourage believers to remain unwed; however, these verses are not commands and they are accompanied by provisions for marriage. An example occurs in Corinthians where Paul begins by acknowledging that this letter and these words in particular are in response to questions he was asked.

> "Now for the matters you wrote about: It is good for a man not to marry. But since there is so much immorality each man should have his own wife, and each woman her own husband."
> (1 Corinthians 7:1 - 2)

Paul continues on in verses 8 and 9 to answer the question about the unmarried and widows. Again he offers the preferred alternative yet also encourages marriage over the sin of lust.

> "Now to the unmarried and the widows I say : It is good for them to stay unmarried, as I am. But if they cannot control

themselves, they should marry, for it is better to marry than to burn with passion." (1 Corinthians 7:8 - 9)

When Paul writes to the Corinthians again in his second letter he certifies from where his knowledge comes.

"Not that we are competent in ourselves, but our competence comes from God." (2 Corinthians 3:5)

What Paul tells the Corinthians is that he is called to proclaim the Word God has set forth. He confesses to not being competent in himself to direct the followers of Christ but redirecting the attention towards God Himself who pours out His grace and wisdom on those who seek Him. Does man have a better plan than God for restricting marriage in a church? Does man have a new and improved plan for leading man in a personal relationship with the Lord? Celibacy has been difficult for the Catholic church to maintain; it's easier by doctrine than by practice. Unfortunately, Catholic priests who do stumble are treated as the problem rather than the doctrine itself. Many other Catholic priests leave their churches and ministries; but, those numbers are not well publicized. The magnitude of the problem of choosing man's way over God's way is hidden from the membership of the Catholic church.

## But the More Recent Popes Are Better, Right?

The reader may counter at this point. Even if some of those events did take place a thousand years ago, today the papacy is a holy loving office worthy of the first pope, whoever it may have been.

Do not the modern popes, even since Vatican II, endorse the teachings of the church? Do they not subscribe to the notion that the Catholic church is the only true church? Do they sustain they who sat upon Peter's throne? Pius IV in the "Profession of the Tridentine Faith", Article 10 serves to remind even modern popes of the allegiances of their bishops to serve the pope.

"I acknowledge the holy Catholic Apostolic Roman Church for the mother and mistress of all churches; and I promise and swear true obedience to the Bishop of Rome, successor to St. Peter, Prince of the Apostles, and Vicar of Jesus Christ." [6], page 209

Our ultimate accountability is not to the Bishop of Rome (the pope) or anyone else of this life. Rather, our accountability is to the same Christ to whom the church is accountable. Ephesians were reminded of this principle when Paul compared the head of the household to the head of the church.

> "For the husband is the head of the wife as Christ is the head of the church, his body, of which he is the Savior. Now as the church submits to Christ, so also wives should submit to their husbands in everything." (Ephesians 5:23 - 24)

Most often these verses are used to remind wives of their responsibility to yield to the husband. Peter makes this clear even in the cases when the husband is a non-believer (1 Peter 3:1). A more careful review of these verses also reveals that the church is the body of Christ and it is accountable to its head who is none other than Christ himself. No human substitute or institution can claim this authority or succession.

Let's examine one lesson that Peter taught us in Acts.

> "As Peter entered the house, Cornelius met him and fell at his feet in reverence." (Acts 10:25)

Peter made him get up stating:

> "Stand up, I am only a man myself." (Acts 10:26)

How does this lesson serve as an example to the custom of bowing before and kissing different limbs of the pope. Is this Scriptural behavior? Isaiah and then Paul, too, told us in Philippians.

> "that at the name of Jesus every knee should bow, in heaven and on earth and under the earth." (Philippians 2:10)

Both the New and Old Testaments present specific instruction in the ways we are to act before man and before God! In Oswald Chambers classic My Utmost for His Highest [7], for February 24 we are admonished that Paul attracted followers to Jesus, not to himself.

The papacy continues to struggle today amid allegations of financial mismanagement, exorbitant spending to maintain itself, and balancing its teachings with its expectations of strict obedience and conformance. Some examples include:

- John Paul II notified Catholic scholars that public attacks on the official teachings of the church will not be tolerated. One respond drew the comment "It's (the document) an embarrassment." [8]

- More than 10,000 priests have left the priesthood since Second Vatican Council. [9]

- The replacement of "Father" Vincent O'Keefe by John Paul with "Father" Paolo Dezza in 1979.

- Six years after contraceptives were outlawed by Paul VI, less than one in seven US Catholics agreed.

- Upon visiting the US in 1987, the pope was advised that in the past 30 years church attendance had dropped from 75 to 53 percent.

- Archbishop Hunthausen (of Seattle) was told "secretly" that he was being stripped of his authority in several areas because of non-conformances (Bishops take an oath "to maintain, defend, increase and advance the rights, honours, privileges and authority of their Lord the Pope".)

- Many who monitor the teachings of the Catholic church ask the question "How can Catholics eat meat on Fridays today when they were condemned (for the same act) before the Second Vatican Council?" "And how can such reforms occur in light of papal decrees and implied endorsements? [10]

- Brazil, a Catholic stronghold in South America greeted the pope in 1991 with the following statistics:

  - of Brazil's 150 million people (predominantly Catholic) only 8 million Catholics attend church on Sunday, 20 million "Protestants" attend church

  - in Brazil, the Catholic church has about 14,000 priests being outnumbered by "Protestant" pastors by about 3:1

  - over one-half of a million Catholics convert to Protestantism each year!

- Expenses to operate the Vatican in 1992 are expected to reach 180 million dollars; almost one-half, 83 million of which is a forecasted deficit; these costs to support the Vatican Palace and its 10,000 rooms. [11]

- On December 17, 1991, US Catholic bishops voted to eliminate the Mass "obligation" on January 1, August 15, and November 1, if they occur on a Saturday or a Monday. Vatican approval is needed. (See Leviticus 23 for a list of the Lord's holy days and to whom they apply.)

- In a story released by the Associated Press in December of 1991, concerns were being raised in Mexico wherein the Catholic church dominates. Concerns were raised as changes to the constitution were being reviewed including formal state recognition of the Catholic church. (Recall the misuse of power in Rome.)

- Allegations have surfaced concerning the involvement and membership of the papacy in Free Masonry—a forbidden brotherhood according to Rome's teachings. [12]

- "American Catholics are more likely to follow their own conscience or personal preference than to assent unquestionably to papal announcements." [13]

The papacy today is confronted with many issues of importance to the Catholic church and its members. My prayer is for solely (souly) Scripture-based doctrines from the papacy, more reform towards acknowledgments of passed reliance on man's tradition, and a refocus on the teachings of the Bible.

The doctrine of infallibility was adopted on July 18, 1870, at Vatican Council (I) with many participants fearing loss of their own ministries if they decided not to follow the mood of the council. This doctrine applies when the pope is speaking on matters of the church; however, Peter, the first pope according to Catholicism, was rebuked by Paul.

> "When Peter came to Antioch, I opposed him to his face, because he was clearly in the wrong." (Galatians 2:11)

The doctrine of infallibility presents still another opportunity for tradition to take precedence over Scripture. I'll continue to remain with the Scripture.

To summarize and finish this discussion of Peter, Principal or Principle I leave with the following considerations:

- When we place our attention in Peter or a pope, does it turn our attention away from Christ? Is this really God's plan?

- Does our focus on the papacy become a supplement or a replacement for our own salvation through Jesus? Do we recognize that there is no other path according to John 14:6?

- Does following the example of the papacy over the past two thousand years really model a walk with Christ?

I must admit that I have prematurely minimized my attention on the popes. I found the material very disturbing and upsetting. I do not want to dwell on this subject matter but instead think of the goodness and greatness of God. I prefer His majesty over man's misery. Paul reminds us that we should dwell on the good.

> "Finally, brothers, whatever is true, whatever is noble, whatever is right, whatever is admirable–if anything is excellent or praiseworthy–think about such things." (Philippians 4:8)

Does our obedience to the pope (see the oath above required of Catholic bishops) border on breaking the first commandment? Who is first in our lives? Who else do we dare call Lord? Our God expects our allegiance to be with Him and I would be careful to provoke His jealousy in this matter. I'll close this chapter with a lesson from Christ as recorded by the apostle Luke.

> "While all the people were listening, Jesus said to his disciples, 'Beware of the teachers of the law. They like to walk around in flowing robes and love to be greeted in the marketplaces and have the most important seats in the synagogues and the places of honor at banquets. They devour widows' houses and for a show make lengthy prayers. Such men will be punished most severely'." (Luke 20:45)

### Three things you should know after reading this chapter.

✟ Jesus loves you. "Abba", the Aramaic for "father." When Jesus spoke, He spoke Aramaic. When Jesus called to the Father, He called "Abba." Call on Him today; Abba, Father. Explore the relationship He seeks with each of His children. Come unto Him as a child lest you not find the kingdom of God!

✟ Jesus seeks a relationship with you. The head of the church is Christ (Ephesians 5:23). Through Christ, God poured out His love to us. Jesus did not encourage us to add to His laws; instead, the Scriptures warn against adding or removing anything. The best relationship you will ever have is with the Lord. The best vehicle for this relationship is through directly approaching Him. Our relationship with Him necessarily precludes reaching Him through genealogies of man-appointed rulers.

✟ Jesus wants you to love your brothers. The Church that keeps its eyes on the real Father needs no other authority. When you share Christ with those you know, seek His intercession. When you love your brother, do so as Christ commanded—in His name and for His glory.

References

[1] Peter De Rosa, <u>Vicars of Christ</u>: The Dark Side of the Papacy, Crown Publishers

[2] Henry H. Halley, <u>Halley's Bible Handbook</u>, Zondervan Publishing House

[3] Jerrold M. Packard, <u>Peter's Kingdom: Inside the Papal City</u>, Charles Scribner's Sons

[4] <u>The New American Bible</u>, Catholic Bible Publishers, 1970

[5] "DIAL-A-POPE," <u>People of God</u>, June/July 1992

[6] Philip Schaff, <u>Creeds of Christendom: With a History and Critical Notes</u>, Harper & Brothers, Franklin Square, 1896

[7] Oswald Chambers, <u>My Utmost for His Highest</u>, Dodd, Mead & Company, Inc., 1935

[8] "Drawing the Line on Dissent," <u>Time</u>, July 9, 1990, Richard N. Ost

[9] <u>Time</u>, May 24, 1976

[10] "Roman Catholicism," Ron Carlson, a cassette tape available from Cultivate Ministries, Colorado Springs, Colorado

[11] "The Vatican suffers financial woes," <u>People of God</u>, June/July 1991, "Most Rev." Robert F. Sanchez

[12] "Freemasonry and Catholicism," Jim Shaw, a cassette tape available from Cultivate Ministries, Colorado Springs, Colorado

[13] "What Think Ye of Rome," <u>Christian Research Journal</u>, Winter 1993, Kenneth R. Samples

Other Suggested Readings

Alexander Hislop, "The Pagan Origin of Purgatory," Mission to Catholics International

Mark Pena, "From Rome to Christ," Mission to Catholics International

W. A. Criswell, "The Bones of Peter," Mission to Catholics International

L. H. Lehmann (former Roman Catholic Priest), "Priests and Ex-Priests," Mission to Catholics International

"Peter and the Pope," Alpha and Omega Ministries, Phoenix, Az.

Frank Eberhardt, "I Wanted to Serve God as a Priest," Mission to Catholics International

Bartholomew F. Brewer (former Roman Catholic Priest), "The Conversion of a Catholic Priest," Mission to Catholics International

# Chapter 4

## Mary–What Have They Done to You?

> *In the same way, the Spirit helps us in our weakness. We do not know what we ought to pray for, but the Spirit himself intercedes for us with groans that words cannot express.*
> *(Romans 8:26)*

This chapter will examine a number of beliefs centered on Mary, the mother of Jesus. Some of those beliefs include the so called immaculate conception of Mary, the ascension of Mary, the perpetual virginity of Mary, the veneration of Mary, and the intercession of Mary. Every person should have a clear and Scriptural account of Mary's role while recognizing other speculation or conjecture outside of Scripture has no positive impact on our relationship with Christ.

Before reviewing the list of subjects above, please note I present Mary as the mother of Jesus not the mother of God. Our power of reason could lead us through the following assertions and to its apparently logically conclusion:

Mary was the mother of Jesus.

Jesus is God.

Therefore, Mary is the mother of God.

The origin and tradition that Mary was the mother of God dates back to the early Christian church at Ephesus. Ephesus was one of the great centers of pagan worship during the times of the early church. Its patron goddess was Artemis (Greek), also known as Diana to the Romans. This goddess was portrayed as having a multitude of breasts on her front torso. How unsurprising then that Mary was declared the mother of God, in this early capital of paganism, not by early church fathers during her lifetime, not during the early churches during the first centuries of Christianity, but instead at a council in 431. The site of this council is not coincidental. The council was known as the Council of Ephesus, named after its location.

Please search throughout the entire Catholic version of the Bible. Mary is not referred to as the Mother of God anywhere in the Scriptures of that book. Since Jesus pre-existed prior to Mary, and since all things were made by Him and for Him, we recognize that Mary bore the incarnate Jesus or the Christ in the flesh.

Everyone alive on the earth today can trace their ancestries back to two common mothers. Obviously through Eve all human kind was born directly or indirectly with the exception of Adam; whom God Himself formed from the earth. Since the flood of Noah's time, each person must also carry a common relationship to Noah's wife who bore all of the surviving men of the flood, with one exception again, this time Noah.

Believers in Christ share a common spiritual mother in at least one sense. Her description is found in Galatians.

> "Now you, brothers, like Issac, are children of promise. At that time the son born in the ordinary way persecuted the son born by the power of the Spirit. It is the same now. But what does the Scripture say? "get rid of the slave woman and her son, for the slave woman's son will never share in the inheritance with the free woman's son." Therefore, brothers, we are not children of the slave woman, but of the free woman." (Galatians 4:28 - 31)

Paul describes the son born in the ordinary way whereas Sarah offered her slave woman who bore Ishmael. Paul also describes the one born of the Spirit; promised by God to an aged woman at 90. Paul concludes by reminding us that we are children of the free woman and that we will share in the inheritance.

In the three preceding examples, three Scriptural accounts for an ancestral motherly affiliation were offered. Two are physical. One is spiritual. Yet still, we are not encouraged to offer special prayers to or for these women either, despite their contributions to God's promises and eventually, Christianity.

The Catholic church continues to teach the dogma of the immaculate conception of Mary; i.e., Mary was born without sin. Let's look first at a Scriptural account of sin. Paul tells us that no man is perfect.

> "for all have sinned and fall short of the glory of God and are justified freely by his grace through the redemption that came by Christ Jesus" (Romans 3:23 - 24)

These verses tell us two key truths about this subject. First, 'all' have sinned and 'all' fall short of God's glory. Please note that no exceptions are made regardless of any applied man-made status. Second, 'all' are justified through Christ; again, no exceptions that we may be justified through any other tradition or entity. The prophet Isaiah reminds us of two key points in the next verse. His words were as true in his day as they remain today (and every day in between). First, that we have all wandered from the Lord at some time. Second, all our inequities were placed upon Him!

> We all, like sheep, have gone astray, each of us has turned to his own way; and the Lord has laid on him the iniquity of us all. (Isaiah 53:6)

What was Mary's understanding about the nature of salvation? Mary knew she was born with sin and needed salvation. Mary testifies to this regard.

> "And Mary said: 'My soul glorifies the Lord and my spirit rejoices in God my Savior'," (Luke 1:46 - 47)

Mary recognizes, as should we, that she too needs a savior. She does not pretend to be exalted 'above' others; Mary was exalted 'among' others. How wonderful a testimony Mary provides. How wonderful her life must have been with Jesus and Joseph. We find her at the wedding in Cana as she encourages Jesus to do something about the shortage of wine; her encouragement leading to Jesus' first recorded miracle. Mary was there at the cross when Jesus was crucified and when Jesus committed her to the apostle John. She was available as a willing servant through whom the Holy Spirit planted the seed of the Son. None of these events however, in any way support her own birth without sin or her own perfection or her own special power. Jesus even spoke of those who knew Him as His mother and brother conveying their importance as members of a spiritual family over traditional family membership.

Again it is written in Romans.

> "As it is written: 'There is no one righteous, not even one';" (Romans 3:10)

Not even ONE, NOT even ONE. NOT EVEN ONE. This Scripture too was written during or after Mary's time. As well versed as Paul was with the law and the life of Christ, he certainly would have known if Mary was immaculate. (Mary's assumed immaculate state is also thought to necessarily include her mother; however, Catholic teaching is unsure of Mary's grandmother's "state." Just in case you are trying to keep the genealogies and origin of sinlessness straight.)

Contrast how Mary professed her need as a sinner for the Savior with the following Catholic prayer:

## "To Immaculate Mary"

> "You are all fair, O Mary, the original stain is not in You. You are the glory of Jerusalem, You, the joy of Israel, You, the great honor of our people, You, the advocate of sinners. O Mary, O Mary, Virgin most prudent, Mother most merciful, pray for us, intercede for us with our Lord Jesus Christ."

A number of observations can be drawn from this short prayer. First, according to the Bible, 'original stain' is in all of us; Mary included. Second, the glory of Jerusalem and the joy of Israel are its God; Mary is not a god. Third, there is only one intercessor between man and He is God, Christ Jesus. This truth is found in First Timothy 2:5 and the subject is further addressed in the section on Mary as intercessor.

Do we find words that tell us that Mary was born without sin in the Bible? While I have not found them, here's another example of where man's tradition can be placed ahead of the Word of God.

I'm not the first person to question the role of Mary in the church. Nor am I the first to question her declared immaculate conception. Actually, a number of early church bishops and later-to-be-designated saints rejected this doctrine. In addition, a number of "infallible" popes also rejected this doctrine.

The ascension of Mary into heaven is another teaching of the Catholic church. The rationale for this teaching is Mary's exalted position as Jesus' mother, and that therefore it is only logical that she share in ruling with Him from her own throne. Because of her exalted position, Mary can be used as an intercessor as well as a savior, or so the Catholic church teaches.

What does the Bible teach about Mary's ascension? We can find the account of Christ's ascension in Acts 1:9. Revelation describes that Christ will come again descending from the heavens. Ascension and "descension" are not limited to the New Testament. Enoch and Elijah ascended into the sky in the Old Testament. Other Scriptural references use the word "ascend" to describe traveling or "going up to" another place, or smoke ascending up into the sky, and angels ascending and descending.

Mary's ascension however is not found anywhere in the Bible. The Catholic church admits this truth but uses human reasoning to alter the foundation of Biblical teaching. Mary lived her final days with the apostle John (after returning from his exile on Patmos). John outlived Mary. Both of their graves are located in the ancient city of Ephesus. Interestingly, the Bible does not record any account of John's knowledge of Mary's ascension, despite the fact that John wrote his epistles and Revelation almost at the end of the first century–well over a hundred years from Mary's birth.

Three characteristics stand out when I think of Christ's ascension. First, it was prophesied. Jesus told His apostles He would leave them, but promised them the Holy Spirit. Second, Jesus' ascension was visible. In Acts 1:9 "he was taken up before their very eyes." No one who saw this departure would soon forget it. Those present would carry that experience with them forever! Praise God! Third, His ascension was physical. Again, Acts 1:9 tells us "he was taken up" and not His spirit, His image, or any other carefully worded assertion. Fourth, it was purposeful. Christ left so that the Holy Spirit might come and provide power and completed knowledge about how we are to live our lives. Fifth, His ascension contained a promise.

> "'Men of Galilee,' they said, 'why do you stand here looking into the sky? This same Jesus, who has been taken from you into heaven, will come back in the same way you have seen him go into heaven'." (Acts 1:11)

Wow! He's coming back and from the sky and every eye will see Him. And He will place His foot upon the Mount of Olives after the great trumpet call. This hope is my hope for each and every day.

How do these five examinations relate to Mary's purported ascension? First, her ascension was not prophesied. Second, the Bible does not record anyone witnessing this event. Third, while I have not examined the site, I would expect to find Mary's remains still in Ephesus, void of any physical resurrection or subsequent ascension. Fourth, Mary's ascension serves absolutely no purpose in the life of a Christian. A Christian's life is Christ-centric or Christ-centered. Mary's ascension could be used by the evil one (who's been sinning since the beginning (1 John 3:8)) to deceive, mislead, confuse (since there is no confusion through Christ), or divide believers. None of these results are God's intentions for His children. Fifth, Mary's ascension contains no promise for her return, or her intercession, or her intervention. Any belief in such a fulfillment would violate God's Word, abrogate His promises, and compromise His supreme and all atoning sacrifice.

As a final shadow of doubt to be cast upon the ascension of Mary, I would like to emphasize this teaching was not part of the early church. It wasn't adopted after Mary would have ascended. This doctrine became official in the year 1950 by Pius XII about 1900 years after Mary's death.

The Bible presents us with a complete truth and a sufficiency for developing our relationship with Jesus Christ. The rationalization of Mary's exalted role above man and by man is an add-on, a different gospel, a false teaching, and a sin of presumption.

## Mary as Intercessor

The Catholic church proclaims Mary's "powerful intercession has rescued Christians from disaster throughout history, especially when sought through her Rosary." [1] Why would anyone pray to someone else to intercede with our Lord if we have direct access to the Lord? Why would anyone pray to the dead (physically speaking) for those who are still alive? What does the Bible teach us about contacting the dead?

"Let no one be found among you who sacrifices his son or daughter in the fire, who practices divination or sorcery, interprets omens, engages in witchcraft, or casts spells, or who is a medium or spiritist or who consults the dead. Anyone who does these things is detestable to the Lord, and because of these detestable practices the Lord your God will drive out those nations before you." (Deuteronomy 18:10 - 12)

A good application of the consequences of disregarding God's Word can be found in Samuel when Saul attempts to contact the dead about the living.

"Samuel said, 'Why do you consult me, now that the Lord has turned away from you and become your enemy? The Lord has done what he predicted through me. The Lord has torn the kingdom out of your hands and given it to one of your neighbors—to David. Because you did not obey the Lord or carry out his fierce wrath against the Amalekites, the Lord has done this to you today. The Lord will hand over both Israel and you to the Philistines, and tomorrow you and your sons will be with me'." (1 Samuel 28:16 -19)

During the last days of Saul's life, he actually did a number of things wrong in contacting the dead. The following verses are all found in First Samuel 28. In verse 5 Saul was terrified (faithless) of his situation. In verse 6, Saul was impatient in waiting for the Lord to answer him. In verse 7, Saul was disobedient and contacted a medium. In verse 8, and as confirmed in verse 12, Saul used deception and disguised himself to hide his sin in seeking a medium. In verse 15, Saul contacting of the dead annoys Samuel. In verse 16, Saul attempts to draw Samuel into his problems. In verse 19, Saul is told he will die tomorrow. (Don't let anyone deceive you that Romans 6:23 is wrong. The wages of sin is certainly death and not just a physical death!) First Chronicles summarizes Saul's sin.

"Saul died because he was unfaithful to the Lord; he did not keep the word of the Lord and even consulted a medium for guidance, and did not inquire of the Lord." (1 Chronicles 10:13 - 14)

Apparently, Saul died for using a medium and putting his faith in someone else. More importantly, he did not inquire of the Lord! He did not inquire of the Lord! He did not inquire of the Lord! Is three times enough? He did not inquire of the Lord! Saul used another intercessor.

Leo XII, one of the infallible popes, and speaking on behalf of matters for and of the church, in 1891, said we could only approach Christ through Mary for she is co-redeemer. So much for the personal relationship that Jesus said we must have in John 14:6

> "I am the way and the truth and the life. No one comes to the
> Father except through me." (John 14:6)

Either the pope is right, or Jesus is right. I've heard about the popes and I've heard about Jesus. I'll take Jesus!!! If I was to paraphrase the above Scripture negatively it might sound like this: No one else is the way. No one else is the truth. No one else leads to life. Everyone comes unto the evil one through every other entity other than me. Of course Christ spoke and John captured the perfection of this concept. Its negative restatement may trigger a different reaction but hopefully the same conclusion.

Gregory, also an infallible pope, said we are sons of God through Mary. Again, the Bible tells it a little differently where it is written:

> "Therefore, brothers, we are not children of the slave woman
> (Hagar), but of the free woman (Sarah)." (Galatians 4:31)

Sometimes I must admit to being amazed at science and mankind. We've had the completed Bible now for almost two thousand years. Keeping this is mind, a few of years ago it was announced on the news that researchers at a major university had just discovered a common gene found in all humankind indicated that we must all have had the same mother at some point. This theory was also known as the "African Eve" a woman who lived 200,000 years ago. Wow! I'm surprised that someone would fund that research given that Bible believers had all the evidence they needed in Genesis 4. Does that gene come from Eve? Does that gene come from Noah's wife? Not to poke fun at the scientists of the world, but I prefer to have the 'grace gene,' the one that comes from God's blessings and is one indirectly referenced in Galatians. Maybe somebody left something out of the Bible; you know the phrase, where we are sons through Mary. I'll take the Bible as is. Its promise is Jesus Christ and eternity through His redemption and His redemption only.

How specifically does the Catholic church endorse the adoration of Mary? Can anyone substantiate that Mary is exalted above man. Let's examine one of the prayers found in the Catholic <u>New American Bible</u> [1].

## Consecration to Mary

(Recite Hail Mary and add to it the following:)

> "My Queen! my Mother! I give you all myself, and to show my devotion to you, I consecrate to you my eyes my ears, my mouth, my heart, my entire self. Wherefore, O loving Mother, as I am your own, keep me, defend me, as your property and possession."

Here are just a few observations related to the above prayer.

1.  Mary is not a queen, but let's talk about someone who was a queen. *Queen of Heaven* is a phrase used in Jeremiah 7:18 as well as in Jeremiah 44. Written hundreds of years before Mary's existence, this phrase is not a prophecy about the birth of Jesus. The phrase is used instead to depict an important goddess in Babylon. Jeremiah writes to tell us

> "The children gather wood, the fathers light the fire, and the women knead the dough and make cakes of bread for the Queen of Heaven. They pour out drink offerings to other gods to provoke me to anger. But am I the one they are provoking? declares the Lord. Are they not rather harming themselves, to their own shame?" (Jeremiah 7:18 - 19)

Later in Jeremiah 44 the phrase is found several more times.

> "We will not listen to the message you have spoken to us in the name of the Lord! We will certainly do everything we said we would: We will burn incense to the Queen of Heaven." (Jeremiah 44:17)

> "'When we burned incense to the Queen of Heaven and poured out drink offerings to her, did not our husbands know that we were making cakes like her image and pouring out drink offerings to her'?" (Jeremiah 44:19)

> "Because you have burned incense and have sinned against the Lord and have not obeyed him or followed his law or his

decrees or his stipulations, this disaster has come upon you."
(Jeremiah 44:23)

Is it a coincidence that warnings about the Babylonian goddess refers to
the phrase Queen of Heaven? Is it a coincidence that this title has been
transferred to Jesus' mother? Are there adequate warnings or reason for
suspicion regarding Mary's exalted role?

2.   Mary is not my mother, God knew me before I was born, even when
     I was carried in my mother's womb and even since the beginning of
     time. God gave me as a gift to my own mother. Mary is not my
     spiritual mother either. I do appreciate what Mary did in bringing
     forth the physical manifestation of Jesus Christ. I am saved by His
     blood and His blood only. I have a Father and savior and there is no
     other name under all heaven through which man can be saved (Acts
     4:12).

3.   No consecration can I offer to any entity other than my God. My
     God is a jealous God. I am to have no other 'god' beside Him. The
     blood of Jesus Christ is all sufficient and the only true light in the
     world. Anything that interferes, detracts, or supplements His blood
     is a work of the enemy. Know ye not that your body is the temple
     of the Holy Spirit? How dare we consecrate it or any part of it with
     idolatry.

4.   The protection and provision of Jesus Christ is all sufficient. We
     need no other deity to supplement His omnipotence. Don't open
     yourself to possession by any other entity. Remember that Satan
     himself masquerades as an angel of light. Satan, God's most
     beautiful creation is the master of deception; he will do anything to
     draw your attention away from Christ to lead you down the wrong
     path.

Let's examine another prayer in the same book.

## Act of Consecration of the United States to Our Blessed Mother

"Most Holy Trinity; Our Father in Heaven, who chose Mary as
the fairest of your daughters; Holy Spirit who chose Mary as
your spouse; God the Son, who chose Mary as your Mother; in
union with Mary, we adore your majesty and acknowledge
your supreme, eternal dominion and authority. ..."

Mary has no dominion or authority as defined in the Bible.   All of Mary's power comes from the traditions of the church.   The traditions of the church is man's plan of salvation.   Man's plan of salvation came from man's attempt to be like God.   This plan first formed in the Garden of Eden.   Its main characters were Eve and the serpent.   But this plan and man's traditions are not God's plan.   God's plan is found in His Word.   Follow Him.   He is the way, the truth, and the life!

As portrayed in the Story of the Rosary, also included in this Bible, is the following quotation: "Every day of the year, throughout the world, millions of people recite the Rosary in obedience to the Blessed Virgin's many requests ...".   The first commandment tells us who we are to worship.   The first four commandments describe our obedience in our relationship to God.   The last six commandments describe our obedience to God with other people.   No commandment describes any obedience towards Mary.   We don't owe any obedience to Mary and Mary told others to do what He told them to do.   This truth is self-evident at the wedding feast in Cana.   Mary told others to obey Jesus.   She never hinted that in anyway we should obey her or pay homage to her.

As I put these words together, I am reminded of an incident in 1990 when in a church its members were being encouraged to acknowledge and participate in Earth Day.   The priest told the congregation to acknowledge the earth as our "mother" because our body "elements" were found in the earth and would someday return to the earth.   No mention was made of the soul or spirit of a person, just the natural occurrences of the physical death.   We were then told that we should care for the earth just as the earth takes care of us.

While the earth is one of God's instruments through which He provides for us, I cannot fathom the earth as either a person or a mother.   (The use of the phrase "mother earth or earth mother" extends well into the history of the pagan religions of the world.)

As part of the same sermon, the congregation was told they evolved from monkeys.   The likeness of the appendage of the human thumb with that of monkeys' was the only evidence of this evolutionary stance presented.   When the service ended I approached the priest for, unknown to me at that time, that service would be my last at that church.   When I asked the priest about his position on evolution and treatment of the earth he got very loud and put his finger within an inch of my face as if to intimidate me.   Several of the members leaving the service stopped as if they expected a physical confrontation to erupt.   I was really disappointed by his reaction and he seemed to respond as if his ego and teachings were in question.

My disappointment was not diminished when I called the pastor of the church during the week to ask about the incident. I do not even remember today if the pastor said he had or had not heard about the incident but he did say that he had little oversight in what was actually being preached (in his own church)! The major source of continued disappointment stemmed from what he said next and that was that the Catholic church has accepted evolution as an appropriate teaching within the church as long as the Catholic believes that God was the source of the evolutionary process! Wow! Now, the church had yielded to the knowledge of man, once again. (This position assumes that one can consider information concerning evolution–an unproven theory and in reality, with many of its early beliefs already disproven–to be knowledge.)

In this Bible's [1] Introduction to <u>Beautiful Marian Prayers</u> the following short prayer is found:

> "God the Father, God the Son, and God the Holy Spirit alone, do we adore. But next to the triune of God, of all the saints, we venerate most the Mother of God. Inestimably honored by God while on earth, she has been exalted in Heaven."

The following text is located in the "Life of the Blessed Mary" as told in the New American (Catholic authorized version) Bible.

> "Because Mary had been preserved free from sin, it was not fitting that her body should undergo corruption. It was also fitting that she should be the first of the redeemed to share completely in the victory of the Son over sin and death. After her death, she was taken body and soul to heaven. She is the first human to share in the resurrection of Christ. This privilege is called the 'Assumption'."

Again, I encourage the reader to determine whether these words are consistent with those in Scripture since the Catholic church also acknowledges that the words are not found in Scripture.

## Mary's Perpetual Virginity

The Catholic church teaches that Mary was a virgin even after she gave birth to Jesus. In light of Biblical evidence this teaching is hard to reconcile. First, the book of James was written by a man who was believed to have been the brother of Jesus. This same James was thought to be the head of the church in Jerusalem; he was not the apostle James. Second, the book of Jude, is also thought to be written by a brother of Jesus. Although Jude is another form of the name Judas and although it was obviously a popular name, this Jude is believed to be Christ's physical half-brother (the closest sibling relationship anyone could have with Jesus!). Third, contrary yet compelling evidence is found in the first book of the New Testament.

> "Coming to his hometown, he began teaching the people in their synagogue, and they were amazed. 'Where did this man get this wisdom and these miraculous powers?' they asked. 'Isn't this the carpenter's son? Isn't his mother's name Mary, and aren't his brothers James, Joseph, Simon and Judas? Aren't all his sisters with us? Where then did this man get all these things?' And they took offense at him." (Matthew 13:54 - 57)

The account here sure sounds like the parents of Jesus. They did live in what is described as His hometown. The people talked about His physical father and mother. The people continued speaking about his brothers and sisters in the same physical sense. The names of Jesus' brothers seem to be the same as the authors of some of the books of the Bible. This usage seems to be the same Jesus since He was the son of Mary and the carpenter and was performing miracles. If Jesus had at least four brothers and sisters too, how then could anyone proclaim Mary a perpetual virgin? Where in any Bible is there any indication that Mary continued through life as a virgin?

Earlier in Matthew is another piece of information that indicates Joseph's faithfulness and obedience. Discouraged about Mary's pregnancy and considering divorcing her to avoid shaming, her Joseph was visited by an angel. In Matthew 1:25 it is written about Joseph "But he had no union with her until she gave birth to a son." The language indicates Joseph waited until after Jesus' birth to have an intimately physical relationship with his wife. Certainly the evidence presented in

Matthew 13 confirms the postponement of and not the abstinence of the relationship between Joseph and Mary.

## Veneration of Mary

The popes, as the vicars of Christ on earth, redirect the focus of adoration from Christ and to Mary. This leadership trickles down to influence the thinking of others in the church. I remember just prior to the last "Marian" year the Archbishop of Santa Fe wrote a letter that was published in at least one of his churches' bulletins. (Though I remember them well, I am intentionally omitting any unnecessary inclusion of names that might point the finger at any one person or "church" in particular; yet, attempting to provide enough of the details to prevent the loss of integrity in the event.)

In his address, the archbishop reminded his "sheep" that during the Marian year we turn our attention away from Jesus and focus on Mary's role. My first reaction was what a horrible way to practice our faith (then as still a Catholic) by looking away from Christ for a year! Somewhat distressed, somewhat confused, I called the archbishop's office. While I could not speak to him directly, I did speak to one of his staff who commented that the words probably did not say what the archbishop had intended and that in any case he would be sure to gently chide the archbishop when he had the opportunity.

Well, perhaps that would have reminded the archbishop to be more sensitive about the words he selected, but the Marian year does little to glorify the Father. Its intention is to glorify Mary. Since I continued with faithful attendance for the weeks that followed, I also know that no retraction was published. Instead, it is possible that many Catholics practiced just as they were told and spent a year turned away from Christ. Some may not have turned back or were confused as to which direction to turn next. Bible-based Christianity does not plant confusion as to which direction to turn; turn directly towards and through Christ for all things.

A recurring comment Catholics hear about Catholicism when approached to join other churches is the tradition of praying to Mary and saints. [2]

The popes, as introduced earlier, shift attention away from Christ. Pius X offered the following about the rosary and its prayers to Mary:

"The Rosary, of all prayers, is the most beautiful, the most rich in grace, the one which most touches the heart of the Mother of God. If you want peace to reign in your home, say the beads there, every day, with your family."

Remember when the apostles asked Jesus to teach them to pray? Jesus responded with:

"Our Father in heaven, hallowed be your name, your kingdom come, your will be done on earth as it is in heaven. Give us today our daily bread. Forgive us our debts, as we also have forgiven our debtors. And lead us not into temptation, but deliver us from the evil one." (Matthew 6:9)

Jesus prayed directly to the Father. Jesus also told us that the things we asked in His name would be answered. Jesus knew Mary; she was His human-form mother. Yet Jesus did not pray to Mary. Jesus prayed to the Father. Jesus did not offer a series of exceptions to His way of praying. He did not say, for one thing pray to Mary, or for a special gift pray to a 'saint.' Please note there was no hierarchy for intercessors, co-sponsors, or special messengers. Clearly the absence of these techniques is because our relationship with Christ is personal; it's one-to-one; it's all sufficient as is His grace. The Lord is my shepherd. Why would I call on a different entity when I have a personal relationship with an omnipotent almighty God?

Pius X is not the only vicar of Christ to lead His flock to worshiping man-made images. The current pope placed a crown on a statue of Mary after thanking and praising her for saving his life. In an article published in the Washington Post on May 14, 1991, Ron Carlson described in a tape released by Cultivate Ministries, how in Fatima, Portugal the pope paid homage to Mary through her statue. Ron also noted that just after the pope survived the attack on his life that he publicly thanked Mary for saving his life. Paul teaches us the Scriptural way to give thanks.

"Do not be anxious about anything, but in everything, by prayer and petition, with thanksgiving, present your requests to God. And the peace of God, which transcends all understanding, will guard your hearts and your minds in Christ Jesus." (Philippians 4:6 - 7)

The obvious focus here is that we present thanksgiving and needs to God himself. The second (and probably equally important) message in the second verse is an assurance that our hearts will be protected and our minds will be protected.  Given the variety of false teachings available in the world today, our minds and hearts need protection—the protection that can only come through Christ himself.

In the final chapter of the final book of the Bible exists a lesson that should remain with us.  In Revelation it is written

> "I, John, am the one who heard and saw these things.  And when I had heard and seen them, I fell down to worship at the feet of the angel who had been showing them to me.  But he said to me, 'Do not do it!  I am a fellow servant with you and with your brothers the prophets and of all who keep the words of this book.  Worship God'!"  (Revelation 22:8 - 9)

In the Old Testament and in the last book of the New Testament we see we are called to worship God and God alone.

Praying to Mary or any saint or object is wrong; a deceptive intrusion for Satan to get a foothold on our lives or our souls.  This deception was described in the chapter on traditions.  One verse here from Colossians can serve as a reminder.

> "See to it that no one takes you captive through hollow and deceptive philosophy, which depends on human tradition and the basic principles of this world rather than on Christ." (Colossians 2:8)

Could the misdirected adoration of Mary just be another ploy of the enemy to steal the soul into his pit?  Read the following words about soul and spirit possession from the book <u>Our Lady Speaks to Her Beloved Priests</u> wherein Mary reportedly says:

> "I will take possession of their lives, and gently I will transform them ... Learn to let yourself be possessed by me, so that everything that you do will be done by me through you.  It is necessary that the Mother act, and I want to act through you."

According to this declaration, Mary wants to possess, in the most literal sense, the life of the reader.  Our commitment as believers in Christ can only be through Him.  The purported statements from Mary could not have been more articulately stated by Satan himself!  This type of trickery was first exploited upon Eve in the Garden.  Please be careful that no one deceives you or leads you astray—away from Christ or His

Word.  As Acts 17:11 reminds us, to examine the Scriptures daily to see if what you are hearing is true.

In still another book, <u>Novena Prayers in Honor of Our Mother of Perpetual Help</u>, the following similar thoughts are expressed:

> "Come to my aid, dearest Mother, for I recommend myself to thee.  In thy hands I place my eternal salvation, and to thee I entrust my soul. ... I fear nothing; not from my sins, because thou wilt obtain for me the pardon of them; nor from the devils, because thou art more powerful than all hell together; not even from Jesus, my Judge, because by one prayer from thee, He will be appeased.  But one thing I fear, that in the hour of temptation, I may through negligence fail to have recourse to thee and thus perish miserably. ..."

Once again the evidence is presented that a non-Biblical belief, one that fails to be validated by word or precept, is really no gospel at all.  Do not be deceived.  Do not be led astray.

As a closing thought for this section and perhaps a transitional opening for the next, remember: we were given a test to know if any spirit is from God himself.  This test is offered by the apostle John.

> "Dear friends, do not believe every spirit, but test the spirits to see whether they are from God, because many false prophets have gone out into the world.  This is how you can recognize the Spirit of God:  Every spirit that acknowledges that Jesus Christ has come in the flesh is from God, but every spirit that does not acknowledge Jesus is not from God.  This is the spirit of the antichrist, which you have heard is coming and even now is already in the world."  (1 John 4:1 - 3)

John reminds us that the spirit of the antichrist is already in the world.  A few verses earlier he tells us that any man who denies the Jesus was the Christ is antichrist.  In this later passage his focus is a little different.  The passing test of a spirit must confess that Jesus Christ has come in the flesh.  I find these words, and any similar wording lacking from the reported apparitions I've studied.  While they don't deny this truth, they don't acknowledge it either.  Some of the messages shared sound contradictory to the Word of Life.

## The Holy Run Around

As a conclusion to this section I recall the name of a column in a local and highly acclaimed Catholic newspaper. The column is entitled "Mary's Go-Round" and it helps me to think about the circumlocuitious approach taught by the Catholic church for reaching Christ. You are told to pray to saints, and to pray to Mary, and pray with others to saints, and to circulate statues of special importance among church members, and to use rosaries and devotionals to Mary, and let's not forget the salvation promised with scapulars. The scapular I hold now in my hand (a piece of cloth, slightly larger than one square inch, with an image sewn to it and a thin "ribbon" like material, all which is worn as a necklace) declares that "whosoever dies wearing this Scapular shall not suffer eternal fire." The words are written across a picture of Mary. And let us not forget that when someone dies, pray some more for their release from Purgatory, and incur suffering on behalf of the departed, and ... I really believe that this set of deceptions is a "holy run around." Paul assured us that:

> "For through him we both have access to the Father by one Spirit." (Ephesians 2:18)

He did so in Romans also.

> "Christ Jesus who died—more than that, who was raised to life—is at the right hand of God and is also interceding for us." (Romans 8:34)

Maybe this is what the "affectionate Uncle Screwtape" implied when in his twelfth letter to Wormwood [3] when assuring that the gradual road is actually the safest road to hell! I've tried to state it clearly and emphatically throughout this chapter. Think of the "red phone", the direct line that once connected (and may still) the White House and the Kremlin. You, who are in Christ, have a direct line to Him. You don't need any operators to intercede. The line is never busy. It's never overcrowded. It's never overwhelmed. And you're never put on hold. Praise God, Amen!

## Reported Appearances of Mary

Given the premise that Christ alone is Christ, Christ alone is our salvation, and Christ alone is holy, what purpose could God have for demonstrating His power and His glory through Mary?  Not to be irreverent in any way with these advertising-originated comparisons but Christ is the "Real Thing," He is the "Real Deal,", He is the right (righteous one) one baby "uh huh."  For Him there is no substitute; nothing better; nothing other.

Now let's examine why an evil force might prefer to demonstrate its power through what seems to be Mary.

1.  It draws our attention away from Christ.

2.  It causes divisiveness in the body of Christ.

3.  It may lead to belief in a salvation outside of God's plan; a deception towards death.

4.  Can you imagine Satan taunting the Lord, much as He did three times after Jesus' fasting in the desert–"You told them, You showed them, You warned them, You taught them, and they still did not listen!"

The books of Revelation, Matthew, Daniel, and First John, are but four of the books reminding us that in the last days one will rise to power who will deceive the masses.  The Antichrist will also be a religious person.  He will be religious, but not holy.  He will lead the people, but not into life.  He will be widely accepted, but only for three and one-half years.  He will work miracles, but they will be at the hands of Satan.  He will proclaim peace, but only until he establishes himself as an idol of worship.

Is it possible Satan would use any available option to deceive God's children.  I think the answer is yes and we are guaranteed the future holds such an event.  According to Scripture, many will come in His name and deceive the masses.  Today there are some 500 self-proclaimed messiahs in the state of California alone!

Is Satan capable of deceiving?  Ask Eve.  Is Satan capable of making evil look good?  Ask Peter about his thinking in Matthew 16:23.  Is Satan capable of abominations in God's Temple?  Ask the Jews about the history of the Temple in Jerusalem.

With those remarks as a preface, I believe any reported sighting of any suspected angel, saint, or Mary, that does not lead its witnesses to or towards Christ is of another religion; that is, of Satan, who is the author of all false religion.  If the appearance, or presence, or apparition, glorifies itself and not the God of the Abraham, Issac, and Jacob, I would issue a serious caution to those who believe in it or through it.

The Christian Research Institute (CRI) provided two excellent articles on the subject of apparitions. These issues were published in the winter and spring of 1991. Within these articles are additional references for the serious student to consider. Further, other appearances are referenced. The CRI, at my request, presented me with several Scripture-based pamphlets and books dealing with cults, Catholicism, and other current topics of interest to concerned Christians. All this took place after I left the Catholic church and wanted to know more about some teachings I had received. The CRI teaches and evaluates based on the written Word. Many of their materials have greatly enriched me. The following appearances, but not evaluations, are based primarily on sightings presented in the articles.

"Our Lady of Guadalupe" has been a part of the Spanish Catholic culture since 1531. This sighting elevated Mary to "Queen of Mexico" by Pope Pius XII in 1945. More recently, in 1979, Pope John Paul II used these words on his pilgrimage to site: "I come to you bearing in my eyes and in my soul the Image of Our Lady of Guadalupe, your Protectrix." His statement redirects attention from Christ.

In 1858, Mary was reported to have made over a dozen appearances in Lourdes, France. The apparition called for the need for prayer and especially the recitation of the rosary. Bernadette, to whom the apparitions appeared, was also urged to offer penance for the conversion of sinners by walking on her knees and eating grass. Lastly, the apparition gave Bernadette three secrets that she was told not to reveal. The apparition, after several appearances and much cajoling did say that she was the "Immaculate Conception." Reports of this sighting were dismissed by the Catholic church (much like today's sightings at Medjugorje are not endorsed by the Catholic church—more on this shortly).

Let's examine some of these requests from the apparition beginning with the recitation of the rosary. The rosary is based on an ancient Hindu practice; its origins are not Christian. Did Christ ever say the rosary or teach it? Did Christ carry a rosary? The answer to the first two questions is no, and no again. Jesus told us not to pray in vain repetition.

"But when ye pray, use not vain repetitions, as the heathen do: for they think that they shall be heard for their much speaking." (Matthew 6:7, KJV)

This advice from Jesus directly contradicts the recitation of the rosary wherein prayers are offered through Mary (an additional misguided teaching) 50 times per citing of the rosary!

Second, Bernadette was told to do penance and eat grass for the conversion of sinners. Scripture teaches us another way.

"No man can redeem the life of another or give to God a ransom for him." (Psalm 49:7)

Scripture also teaches Christ died once for us on the cross and He Himself cried out "It is finished." Might the eating of grass by a young girl save the souls of someone more than or as a supplement to Christ's atonement? Did He not rise again after three days to prove He was the life?

Third, Bernadette was given three secrets to retain. Secrets are a sign of a cult; they are disguised as handshakes, code words, slogans, and rituals. The Bible contains everything necessary for our salvation and understanding of Christ. God determines what things to keep a mystery until His revelation; but, the way to salvation and true life is hardly a secret.

In 1917, Mary was reported to have been seen again; again by children but this time in Fatima, Portugal. The children were told to pray for peace specifically by reciting the rosary-again. Again the children were given secrets to maintain. Yet in this series of visitations, the children were presented with visions of hell (can these be good?). Reportedly during one visit, the sun turned violently, fell, danced over the heads of observers, and then returned to normal. In 1930 the Catholic church formally disapproved the sightings as official. Since then, however, many infallible popes have continued to visit and praise Lady of Fatima.

In 1970, in New York state, a housewife began seeing visions of Mary. The apparition's messages altered the teachings of the Catholic church, especially the then recent changes from Second Vatican Council. The local church officials discounted the sightings as neither miraculous nor sacred and certainly not authentic.

In 1981, a long series of apparitions began in Medjugorje Yugoslavia. These appearances were made to several children who have continued to see them, reportedly daily, for at least ten years. Two of the original witnesses have ceased to continue daily visions and in all the number of visions is approaching 3000. A number of events surrounding these apparitions are reason for concern.

First, during an early appearance the children rushed the vision, fell at its feet and began to pray. The apparition did not rebuke this behavior and tell the children to kneel before and pray to God only. Second, this apparition also relayed secrets to the children. Reportedly, ten secrets in all would be given; some of the children already know all the secrets and others do not. These secrets are to be revealed in the future by the children.

Second, a set of messages was also left with the children. The messages call for faith, praying the rosary, fasting, penance, conversion to God, and peace. Some of these causes appear noble; others were questioned with earlier apparitions. Over one thousand messages have been delivered.

Third, supernatural signs have been reported involving the sun's movement and colors, and others such as the arms of a twenty-foot cement cross spinning or disappearing, healings, and additional visions. While I have no doubt that our almighty God can do all these things and more, local investigators (inside the church) have discounted many of the alleged miracles.

In the May 1992 issue of the Catholic publication People of God from the CNS, reports of shrinking pilgrimages to Medjugorje. Vicka Ivankovic, a 25 year-old and last remaining of the original visionaries, explains the apparition (Mary) "doesn't have the happy smile as she used to have."

A local bishop, Pavao Zanic, continues to dismiss the sightings. He is reported to have caught the visionaries confabulating and exaggerating or developing their own stories and healings. A five-year study with fifteen church officials, concluded that there was no supernatural involvement in the events. Early reports from the visionaries promised five secrets, not ten. In 1981, the children stated the apparition would only appear three more times; this number was off by about 3000! Also in 1981, in response to a question, the apparition declared all religions good before God. The Bible tells us just the opposite especially throughout the first five books written by Moses. This apparition made one more promise; that this would be her last appearance on earth.

(This reported "last appearance" seems to have been shattered by another reported series of sightings occurring over several years in Georgia. These sightings included not only Mary, but Jesus also. Nancy Fowler, who receives the visions, says "I want peace in the world and there's only one place to find it—at the feet of the Blessed Mother." [4] )

Finally, these children have described seeing other visions of angels, Jesus, Satan, deceased relatives, heaven, hell, and purgatory. Contacts, even visual visits with the dead is strictly forbidden by God's law. The Bible teaches us that no man has seen heaven (1 Corinthians 2:9). The Bible does not speak a single word about purgatory. The Bible tells us to resist and flee Satan; these children say Mary brought them face-to-face with Satan. I find these events contrary to God's teachings in the Bible.

And no wonder, for Satan himself masquerades as an angel of light. It is not surprising, then, if his servants masquerade as servants of righteousness. Their end will be what their actions deserve. (2 Corinthians 11: 14 - 15)

I plead with you once more, please don't be deceived.

## Mary—A Redefined Role Under Second Vatican Council

Some outsiders and many insiders of the Catholic church continue to point to the Second Vatican Council as the church's internal reformation; an event of such significance its very occurrence demands a "new look" at the new Catholicism. Thomas Bokenkotter [5] looks at a few of the declarations of the Second Vatican Council concerning Mary. Let's examine a few of them.

> "Mary, indeed is the new Eve, who by total faith and obedience and complete devotion to the person and work of the Son untied the knot bound by the first Eve's disobedience."

Is Mary in any way, anywhere in the Scripture, described as the new "Eve?" To the contrary, we are depicted as children, instead, of Sarah (and not the slave woman) (Galatians 4:31). I believe it was Jesus who untied the knot. Hebrews clarifies:

"And by that will, we have been made holy through the sacrifice of the body of Jesus Christ once for all." (Hebrews 10:10)

The Second Vatican Council took another "new" stance on Mary's role as mediator.

"This mediation of Mary ... is merely the most notable example of the way God enables his creatures to share in his Son's saving work of redemption."

While the Catholic church admits that the doctrines of the Immaculate Conception and the Assumption are not found in Scripture, (see comments on "The Fundamentalist Challenge" in Chapter 7) it pretends to maintain the importance of Scripture in its doctrines.    Clearly Scripture teaches a different concept in the well-known verse from John.

"Jesus answered, 'I am the way and the truth and the life.  no one comes to the Father except through me'."  (John 14:6)

As clear as the preceding Scripture is, Paul described the singularity of the mediator when writing to Timothy.

"For there is one God and one mediator between God and men, the man Christ Jesus,"  (1 Timothy 2:5)

Bokenkotter continues to describe the feeling of the Council:

"The Council warmly recommends devotion to the Blessed Mother of God, which it says has always existed in the church and which need in no way detract from our adoration of the Son, for the two forms of prayer are on totally different levels."

Shortly thereafter and in apparently contradictory language he continues describing the Council:

"Devotion to Mary declined precipitously as old forms of piety disappeared with little replacement.  Rosaries and scapulars were discarded, statues of Mary were removed from many parish churches, old hymns faded from memory, and May Day celebrations disappeared."

Unfortunately, these words were not true universally in the self-ascribed universal church.  The continued adoration of Mary and the distraction from Christ was one of the reasons I surrendered hope of being an instrument of change in the Catholic church. While teaching grade school children in New Mexico's largest Catholic parish I was urged to frequent the garden behind the church where a statue of Mary had been placed. Rosaries were made for and given to the children by the director of the program in celebration of a Marian feast day. Several months of teaching the children about the love and role of Jesus were supplanted, at least in part, by idolatry.

While the Catholic church has made attempts to obscure its harsh pronunciations against non-Catholics it is also active in seeking to widen its appeal within its own congregation. For instance, an article, Historic Statue Renamed To Satisfy N.M. Indians [6], describes the offensive nature of the recently renamed statue from "La Conquistadora" to "Our Lady of Peace." Evidently, the previous name offended the Native American population due to the nature of the cultural conquest. Both Native Americans and non-native Americans have overlooked the nature of idol worship, which continues as a part of the tradition of the Catholic church. It is the latter that both groups should find offensive when compared with the Lord's direct commands concerning the building and the worship of idols made by human hands.

In contrast to the words of the Council, scapulars, rosaries, statues, and other forms of idol worship are alive and well in the Catholic church. An advertisement appears regularly in the People of God Catholic newspaper advertising for scapulars, rosaries, and hope if you have tried everything else in Mary. If all these items of worship were discarded or discouraged by the Second Vatican Council, why do they continue to be so prevalent in circulation today? If these "old forms of piety" were to be discontinued, why are they prominently advertised in Catholic circulations? Has the Catholic church changed its stance on Marian worship? Is this change merely in doctrine but void in practice? Our words and our actions need to be consistent.

Integrity is the enemy of hypocrisy and likewise, hypocrisy the enemy of integrity.

| Three things you should know after reading this chapter. |
| --- |

✟   Jesus loves you. Jesus loves you directly. He does not try to supplement His abundant love through other objects or persons that distract from His relationship with you.

✝ Jesus seeks a relationship with you. The relationship provided for us by the Father, through the Son, and under the power of the Holy Spirit is wholly God's. All power and authority are His and flow from Him in the present and the age to come. A relationship with Him is true and the utmost; accept nothing less than His desire to dwell with you.

✝ Jesus wants you to love your brothers. We know what God is because God is love. When you share the news of the risen Christ with others you share love. When Jesus commissioned the apostles to go forth and spread the Good News, it was about Him, the Way, the Truth, and the Light.

References

[1] The New American Bible, Catholic Bible Publishers, 1970

[2] Patricia Zapor, CNS, "Catholic immigrants find welcome at non-Catholic churches," People of God, August 1992.

[3] The Screwtape Letters, C. S. Lewis, Barbour and Company, Inc., 1990

[4] Michael Browning, "Religious Visions Stir Pilgrims, Doubting Thomases," Albuquerque Journal, 7/25/93

[5] Essential Catholicism, Thomas Bokenkotter, Doubleday & Company, 1985

[6] Tom Sharpe, "Historic Statue Renamed To Satisfy N.M. Indians," Albuquerque Journal, 7/12/92

Other Suggested Readings

"Worldwide Rosary for Life planned," People of God, Fall 1991

Walter Martin, "Charismatics and the Cult of Mary," Parts I and II, Christian Research Institute

Kenneth R. Samples, "Apparitions of the Virgin Mary," Christian Research Journal, Winter 1991 & Spring 1991 (Parts I and II)

CNS, "Lutheran-Catholic dialogue recognizes authentic Marian devotion is not idolatrous", People of God

# Chapter 5

# Selected Doctrines on the Sacraments of Roman Catholicism

Many of us spend time investigating our choices in life. Many of us spend a great deal of time weighing various options when buying a house; location, financing, school systems, size, and neighbors are examples of some of the options. When we consider buying a new car, color, seating, price, manufacturer might be some of the considerations. Even something as mundane as buying gum today requires some thought; flavor, shape, sugar free, and number of pieces all serve as considerations in this purchase decision. Unfortunately, sometimes we spend a lot less thinking about our relationship with God, how to serve Him, how to glorify Him, how to come to know Him better day-by-day.

For many of us, the primary vehicle for our knowing Christ better is our church. The church is a place where we receive feeding about our walk with Him and it is also a place to gather and worship Him with other believers. Churches, just like secular organizations have principles, or by-laws, or value systems that often provide insight into the organization's focus. These insights help us understand the emphasis of doctrinal teaching.

Churches do not offer a relationship with Jesus Christ. Christ has already done that; churches may remind us of that invitation. Churches do not offer eternal salvation. Christ has already done that; churches may remind us of His grace. Churches do not rescue us from eternal separation from God.   Christ has already done that; churches may remind us of the consequence of our decision not to accept Him.   No church saves.   Christ saves.

Individuals have a responsibility to carry forth the Word of God.   The "church" is the body of Christ; it is not an institution of hierarchies and offices.   The "church" is the bride of Christ awaiting His return and remaining faithful to Him.   Churches, composed of people, are then groups of believers.   An effective church must do the work of Christ working to glorify the Father and to save man.   Christ's work is captured in the Bible and not in man's traditions.   When Jesus spoke of the greatest commandment He told us to love the Lord, and to love our brothers.   (1 John 3:23)

In light of this summary evidence, the following is a review of some of the doctrines of the Catholic church.   All of the doctrines listed are part of the active beliefs of the Catholic church today.   The Second Vatican Council endorsed all the writings of the Council of Trent from the 1500s.   As recorded by S. J. Abbott in <u>The Documents of Vatican II,</u> John XXIII acknowledged that the church accepts

> "... all the teachings of the Church in its entirety and preciseness, as it still shines forth in the act of the Council of Trent and First Vatican Council ..."

The Council of Trent convened to respond to the growth of dissension in the church due in part to Martin Luther's questioning of beliefs like purgatory and indulgences.   The Council of Trent was not the first convention of the church to deal with the questioning of its traditions and teachings.   In the early 1400s, the synod of Constance condemned another person for his views and use of Scripture finding him a heretic.   Ten years later and decades after John Wycliffe had died, his bones were exhumed, burned, and thrown into the river.   [1]

The Council of Trent developed a harsh response to the questions of the day and positioned the teachings of Catholicism (an outgrowth of traditions and admitted by the Catholic church) against the teachings of Christ as captured in the Bible.   In all, as I have counted them, over 100 anathemas were issued by the Council against anyone who did not believe in the teachings and traditions of the Catholic church.   Anathemas are curses and damnations to hell; strong language from the self-proclaimed only true "body of Christ."

Many Catholics do not believe those teachings still today. Many Catholics do not realize that they stand accursed by the institution to which they belong. Too often today's Catholic is unaware of the Council of Trent and many other earlier councils that established an unalterable foundation for Catholicism. I have selected but a few of the many decrees from the infamous council hoping to distinguish the difference between the doctrines of tradition and the doctrines of Christ.

The following excerpts from the Council of Trent are found in The Creeds of Christendom, Volume II [2]. This text presents both the Latin and the English translation for the more serious scholar.

The issue of salvation is core to our acceptance and understanding of our almighty God. Look first at this critical issue as recorded in Chapter 15 of the Council of Trent in January of 1547.

"In opposition also to the subtle wits of certain men, who, by pleasant speeches and good words, seduce the hearts of the innocent, it is to be maintained, that the received grace of Justification is lost, not only by infidelity whereby even faith itself is lost, but also by any other mortal sin whatever, though faith be not lost; ..."

These words clearly teach that justification (salvation) can be lost. The question of lost salvation is a divisive issue within denominations. I cannot find in the Bible where salvation can be lost. The opposite can be found in Romans.

"And we know that in all things God works for the good of those who love him, who have been called according to his purpose. For those God foreknew he also predestined to be conformed to the likeness of his Son, that he might be the firstborn among many brothers. And those he predestined, he also called; those he called, he also justified; those he justified, he also glorified. (Romans 8:28 - 30)

These verses do not indicate that anyone "slips through the cracks" once they have been called. While the usage of "predestined" also causes concern among denominations I believe God predestined each and every one of us. His plan of salvation is extended to all. All of us have the opportunity to be called children of God. (See further explanation of God's guarantee in the commentary on Canons 23 and 27 below.)

The above words from the council also indicate justification is lost through mortal sin. The words "mortal sin" are not found together anywhere in the Bible. The word mortal is only used to describe our bodies or flesh and sometimes in the context of sinning but not in the context of one sin being worse than another. The word "venial" is not found anywhere in the Bible. Biblically speaking, only one sin can be considered worse than any others; the unpardonable sin which many Bible teachers believe to be the rejection of the Holy Spirit (see Mark 3:29). The development of mortal sins however does impose excessive guilt if not dealt with by members of the Catholic church.

Canon 27 seems to repeat this same notion that one's salvation can be lost. It also reinforces the concept of mortal sin as taught by the Catholic church but is not in the Bible.

> "If any one saith, that there is no mortal sin but that of infidelity; or, that grace once received is not lost by any other sin, however grievous and enormous, save by that of infidelity: let him be anathema."

Paul addresses our assurance again writing to the believers in Corinth.

> "... But you were washed, you were sanctified, you were justified in the name of the Lord Jesus Christ and by the Spirit of our God." (1 Corinthians 6:11)

Canon 15 on justification continues:

> "If any one saith, that a man, who is born again and justified, is bound of faith to believe that he is assuredly in the number of the predestinate: let him be anathema."

Dr. Bruce Dunn, a minister whose radio ministry I mentioned earlier, once delivered a very powerful message on this topic that had a major impact on me. Dr. Dunn described how we would "know" about our salvation and how the Bible never said we would "feel" saved or "act" saved. The apostle known as the one Jesus loved wrote these words.

> "I write these things to you who believe in the name of the Son of God so that you may know that you have eternal life." (1 John 5:13)

Clearly Canon 15 says that if someone believes by faith with assurance, then he is accursed by the Catholic church. John's first epistle from the

Bible tells us something apparently different. God wants us to know so that we can speak in full confidence of His love and plan.

Canons 18 and 23 are interesting to examine together. They certainly appear to contradict each other.

> "If any one saith, that the commandments of God are, even for one that is justified and constituted in grace, impossible to keep: let him be anathema."

> "If any one saith, that a man once justified can sin no more, nor lose grace, and that therefore he that falls and sins was never truly justified; or, on the other hand, that he is able, during his whole life, to avoid all sins, even those that are venial,–except by a special privilege from God, as the Church holds in regard of the Blessed Virgin: let him be anathema."

If I read these two correctly, the first curses the believer who finds the commandments impossible to keep. Canon 23 curses anyone who believes that they can remain void of sin without God's help. The second point in this second canon implies that anyone who is justified and believes that grace cannot be lost is also cursed. This doctrine contradicts Paul's teaching of the Ephesians.

> "You also were included in Christ when you heard the word of truth, the gospel of your salvation. Having believed, you were marked in him with a seal, the promised Holy Spirit, who is a deposit guaranteeing our inheritance until the redemption of those who are God's possession–to the praise of his glory." (Ephesians 1:13 - 14)

What inspiration and encouragement Paul leaves with us in these verses!

1. We were included in Christ himself.

2. We heard the word of truth.

3. We did our part; we believed!

4. We were identified and sealed in Christ.

5. We have been co-signed for with a deposit and a guarantee until He comes to get us.

6. We live these truths for His glory–not ours.

The example presented in Canon 23, regarding the sinless nature of the "Blessed Virgin" is not taught or alluded to anywhere in the Bible. In the chapter on Mary, counter arguments are suggested asserting Mary's admission of the need for a savior.

Canon 20 places the teachings (traditions) of the church, herein referred to as "commandments" on par with the commandments of God.

> "If any one saith, that the man who is justified and how perfect soever, is not bound to observe the commandments of God and of the Church, but only to believe; as if indeed the Gospel were a bare and absolute promise of eternal life, without the condition of observing the commandments: let him be anathema."

As Christians we are called to obey the commandments. We also believe that the "Gospel" will help us to follow those commandments as we follow its recorded teachings. Accepting Jesus Christ, however, is the all sufficient act necessary for eternal life just as His death on the cross was the all sufficient act necessary for the atonement of our sins. No person can offer any sacrifice greater than the one of Christ Jesus. Fortunately for us, it's an act He already performed so that we can witness its truth.

The Word of God is pure. Knowing Christ and dwelling in His Word is sufficient. No one can be born of God and retain a will to continue sinning. In Psalm 19 David recorded his feelings about God's Word.

> "The law of the Lord is perfect, reviving the soul.
>
> The statutes of the Lord are trustworthy, making wise the simple.
>
> The precepts of the Lord are right, giving joy to the heart.
>
> The commands of the Lord are radiant, giving light to the eyes.
>
> The fear of the Lord is pure, enduring forever.
>
> The ordinances of the Lord are sure and altogether righteous.
>
> They are more precious than gold, than much pure gold; they are sweeter than honey, than honey from the comb.

By them is your servant warned; in keeping them there is great reward." (Psalm 19:7 - 11)

David summarizes by telling us that the Lord's Word is

* a law to be followed;

* perfect; it could not be better!

* worthy of our trust, even making us wise;

* a source of our joy;

* a light for our eyes helping us to see better;

* reliable and completely right before God;

* more valuable than precious metals;

* sweeter than the sweetness of honey; and

* both a warning for His servant and a reward for its keeper.

With the understanding that David displayed, no wonder God knew David as a man after His own heart. John foresaw a great event in the destiny of the believer as described in Revelation.

"I saw heaven standing open and there before me was a white horse, whose rider is called Faithful and True. With justice he judges and makes war. His eyes are like blazing fire, and on his head are many crowns. He has a name written on him that no one knows but he himself. He is dressed in a robe dipped in blood, and his name is the Word of God. The armies of heaven were following him, riding on white horses and dressed in fine linen, white and clean. Out of his mouth comes a sharp sword with which to strike down the nations. "He will rule them with an iron scepter." He treads the winepress of the fury of the wrath of God Almighty. On his robe and on his thigh he has this name written:   KING OF KINGS AND LORD OF LORDS." (Revelation 19:11 - 16)

Canon 21 presents us with still another paradox; this dichotomy however, is also born within the teachings of the Catholic church.

"If any one saith, that Christ Jesus was given of God to men, as a redeemer in whom to trust, and not also as a legislator whom to obey: let him be anathema."

Jesus Christ is the legislator. Jesus Christ is the redeemer in whom we are to trust. I agree with these statements. My confusion however stems from the oaths taken by bishops to obey the pope and not God Himself. My confusion stems from confession to and forgiveness from a priest (more on this later during an examination of the sacrament of confession) rather than the sole mediator (1 Timothy 2:5) and the perpetual intercessor (Hebrews 7:25). My confusion stems from the postulation by the Catholic church that someone else (Mary) can now intercede. Which of these many teachings am I to believe? We must search out the Scriptures daily to see if what we hear is true.

Canon 29 offers the doctrine of the Catholic church regarding justification, baptism, and forgiveness.

> "If any one saith, that he who has fallen after baptism is not able by the grace of God to rise again; or, that he is able indeed to recover the justice which he has lost, but by faith alone without the sacrament of Penance, contrary to what the holy Roman and universal Church—instructed by Christ and his Apostles—has hitherto professed, observed, and taught: let him be anathema."

While the "sacrament of Penance" is investigated later in this chapter we can return again to the criminal on the cross in Luke who was justified by faith alone. While the criminal obviously repented, Luke does not record that his expression of faith was in any way a confession of sin; yet he was apparently forgiven. Luke does not record that the presence of a confessional "box", a ritual of prayer and exchanges between the sinner and the forgiver, nor the customary "three Hail Marys and an Our Father." Ephesians provides another wonderful insight into Paul's teaching concerning this doctrine

> For it is by grace you have been saved, through faith—and this is not from yourselves, it is a gift of God—not by works, so that no one can boast. (Ephesians 2:8)

God's grace is a gift. This gift comes from Christ and not from an institution. Paul states this truth clearly. The Bible does not teach that the Catholic church can implement a plan of salvation based on the "works" of the sacraments.

## Man's Plan Is Not Equal to God's Plan

As a minor diversion into the worldly, I want to demonstrate a similarity between the use of logical comparisons in computer programming languages and the doctrine of grace. Examples of these comparisons include less than, greater than, less than or equal, greater than or equal, and equal. All of these same comparisons also have a negative form, such as, not less than, not greater than, and not equal. The logical comparison that can be applied to salvation is the not equal, often represented in various languages by the abbreviation "NE." A vivid contrast of two approaches not being equal (NE) is Christ's atonement on the cross and our atonement through works (an atonement which is really no atonement at all). The letters "ne" are also the difference in two words that recapitulate the non-equality of two approaches to atonement; those two words are "done" and "do."

Accepting what Christ has "done" for us, the Life provided through Jesus the Son (while simultaneously God also), is quite different from what we attempt to "do" to justify our own righteousness before Him. There's no comparison, no parallel, and no equality (NE) in those two diverse approaches. His atonement is the payment. Our acceptance consummates His perfect covenant. Man cannot devise any plan as a substitute for God's. His ways are perfect. Our very nature is sinful. His way is done. Our ways can never do anything better. His ways promise eternal life. Man's ways promise eternity apart from God. When considering His plan and man's plan, they just are NOT EQUAL.

Canon 30 of the Council of Trent comments further on justification and forgiveness but also introduces Purgatory as an installment plan for earning unity with Christ.

> "If any one saith, that, after the grace of Justification has been received, to every penitent sinner the guilt is remitted, and the debt of eternal punishment is blotted out in such wise that there remains not any debt of temporal punishment to be discharged either in this world, or in the next in Purgatory, before the entrance to the kingdom of heaven can be open: let him be anathema."

The doctrine of Purgatory is not taught in the Bible. The word itself does not appear in the Bible, nor does the concept, nor does the Bible indicate any authority for the Catholic church to champion this doctrine.

The chapter "Peter, Principle or Principal," discusses the origin and teaching of the doctrine of purgatory. To summarize that information I refer to Hebrews.

> "Just as man is destined to die once, and after that to face judgment, so Christ was sacrificed once to take away the sins of many people; ..." (Hebrews 9:27)

Because man is to die once and then be judged, the Catholic church's "parole system" under the jurisdiction of whoever administers Purgatory, is contrary to the teachings of the Bible. Since Christ was sacrificed once to take away sin, how can we accept the notion that we too must pay for those sins? Is our sacrifice more significant the price Christ paid? Are we literally the "Lamb of God" who takes away the sin as proclaimed when John the Baptist introduced Jesus?

## Selected Doctrines Surrounding the Sacraments

The following canons were written to clarify the teachings of the Catholic church regarding the sacraments in general. Although more than one-half of the decrees dealt with the sacraments, once again, only a sampling of the many canons established are presented.

Canon 1 attempts to substantiate the sacraments on the teachings of Christ. This canon establishes the number of proper sacraments at seven.

> "If any one saith, that the sacraments of the New Law were not all instituted by Jesus Christ, our Lord; or, that they are more, or less, than seven, to wit, Baptism, Confirmation, the Eucharist, Penance, Extreme Unction, Order, and Matrimony; or even that any one of these seven is not truly and properly a sacrament: let him be anathema."

Jesus did tell believers to go forth and baptize in Matthew 28. Jesus did tell believers to celebrate "The Lord's Supper" in remembrance of Him in Luke 22. Peter did tell sinners to repent in Acts 2. He did not tell them to do penance. In Matthew 3, John the Baptist did tell his listeners to "repent, for the kingdom of heaven is near."; John did not say to do penance either. The seven sacraments of the Catholic church, as defined and performed, are uniquely those that grew from the traditions of the Catholic church. Which of these seven can you find that Christ himself received either formally or non-ceremoniously? According to the promises of God's Word, which of the seven do you need to ensure eternal companionship with God?  Canon 4 asserts the necessity of the sacraments for salvation.

> "If any one saith, that the sacraments of the New Law are not necessary unto salvation, but superfluous; and that, without them, or without the desire thereof, men obtain of God, through faith alone, the grace of justification;–though all are not indeed necessary for every individual: let him be anathema."

This canon has a serious conflict with the Bible.  Further, this canon has a serious conflict with Jesus' own words.  Many of us remember the two criminals who were to be executed with Jesus.  In Luke's account we find one of the criminals came to know Christ even as the criminal was also being put to death.  Jesus did not say "time out, I've got a baptism to do," or a confirmation, or a series of sacraments.  Jesus did not say "I'll see you after Purgatory".  Jesus did not say "How many mortal sins are you carrying that are unconfessed?"  Jesus simply told the criminal:

> "I tell you the truth, today you will be with me in paradise."
> (Luke 24:43)

If I believed the necessity of works to accomplish God's salvation in my life, I would at least find some small measure of relief in knowing I do not need all the sacraments.  Of course then I'm not really sure of just how many is the right number for me.  Are two enough?  Will three sacraments assure me of less time in Purgatory?  If I only have time for three while there are seven, which ones provide me with the most "points?"  What's the formula for the value of each sacrament?  Should I attempt to receive the Eucharist daily to offset the possibility that I may not receive Extreme Unction at the time of death?  Can I barter three confessions for not receiving Orders?  Where can I find more information on these guidelines in the Bible?  Do answers to any of these questions really exist?

Pius IV writing in the "Profession of the Tridentine Faith", Article 4 asserted

> "I also profess that there are truly and properly seven sacraments of the new law, instituted by Jesus Christ our Lord, and necessary for the salvation of mankind, though not all for every one, ... "

Pius would have delivered to his followers far more insight if he described just how many were "necessary for salvation". Marriage, "Holy Matrimony" is a sacrament, but Catholicism taught that is was better for their priests to remain unmarried and even celibate. Which then is more pleasing to the Catholic church? Why then would both be considered sacramental? Which is more pleasing to God?

Canon 6 refutes the notions of believers at the time just preceding the Council of Trent who described the sacraments, especially baptism, as an outward expression of faith.

> "If any one saith, that the sacraments of the New Law do not contain the grace which they signify, or, that they do not confer that grace on those who do not place an obstacle thereunto; as though they were merely outward signs of grace or justice received through faith, and certain marks of the Christian profession, whereby believers are distinguished amongst men from unbelievers: let him be anathema."

Canon 5 also refutes a precept; that the commandments are expressions of faith whereas the Catholic teaching firmly held (and still does) that the sacraments are a precondition for salvation. See the aforementioned Canon 4.

> "If any one saith, that these sacraments were instituted for the sake of nourishing faith alone: let him be anathema."

Canon 9 reminds members of the Catholic church that certain sacraments can only be received one time.

> "If any one saith, that, in the three sacraments, to wit, Baptism, Confirmation, and Order, there is not imprinted in the soul a character, that is, a certain spiritual and indelible sign, on account of which they can not be repeated: let him be anathema."

For the sake of discussion, let's assume the following situation. A person is separated (by death, misfortune, war, etc.) at an early age (older than the age of baptism but younger than the age at which memory is available) from knowledge of his or her parents. This person wants to practice Catholicism and seeks to be baptized after attending the necessary orientations and proclaiming the right professions. Can this person be baptized in the Catholic church? If the person was already baptized as an infant (as is the common practice), then the sacrament cannot be performed. If the person was not baptized, then they cannot be saved. In addition, according to this canon, if the person believes that it is not important to know whether or not they were once baptized, then they are accursed by the institution from which they seek to be baptized and which they seek to join.

I have presented a "simple" situation with some very serious consequences. The situations could easily become much more complicated. Is Christ's plan really all that complicated? Was our salvation based on faith in Him or our own collection of accomplishments? Consider today whether you will trust Him or you will trust in those who pretend to speak for Him while not consistently presenting His plan.

Canon 10, in an indirect fashion, states that only those authorized (by the Catholic church) can understand the Word and extend to the recipients of the sacraments, God's grace. The close of Matthew 28 directs the eleven "disciples" to go forth into all nations making other "disciples," baptizing them, and teaching them. Evidently, these disciples would then also baptize and teach; as would these new disciples and their disciples and so on. From this commissioning many disciples are brought into the kingdom. Are not these disciples believers? Are not believers disciples? Are not these disciples and believers directed to baptize and proclaim the Word?

> "If any one saith, that all Christians have power to administer
> the word, and all the sacraments: let him be anathema."

On the contrary, Catholics were unable to proclaim the Word. It was unlawful for the Word to be published in the language of the people. It was unlawful for a Catholic to peruse a Bible translated into the language of the people (Protestant Bibles were designated as such). It was unlawful for a Catholic to enter a heretic's church (translation– "Protestant"). The Catholic church maintained that only their anointed could read and share the Word of God. During many of the years that the church maintained this position, many of the anointed of the church were themselves illiterate.

Second Vatican Council did reaffirm that seven sacraments were received from Christ. The Council also forfeited on an opportunity to explain the Scriptural foundation for each of these sacraments.

## Selected Doctrines on the Sacrament of Baptism

The following canons were also delivered at the Council of Trent. These in particular were issued regarding baptism. The wording contained in Canon 5 is poignant to the Christian walk.

"If any one saith, that baptism is free, that is, not necessary unto salvation: let him be anathema."

My first difficulty with this teaching is that it is not based on Biblical understanding; the criminal (thief) at the cross comes quickly to mind—again. What about all the Old Testament saints; Moses, Joseph, Abraham, Job, Daniel, Isaiah and the other prophets? Another covenant one might respond; if so, then the canon needs to be further qualified. If baptism were absolutely critical, why did not the New Testament authors capture the baptism of Mary and all the apostles? I remember in the late 1980s hearing a priest, who was trying to offer comfort to the Catholics attending mass, and telling those in attendance that God would take care of the unbaptized infants who had passed away. No doubt the Catholic priest either has or assumes a wide latitude in delivering sermons that contradict the teachings of the church (which cannot be wrong—more on this later). John teaches something a bit contrary to the canon.

And this is his command: to believe in the name of his Son, Jesus Christ, and to love one another as he commanded us. (1 John 3:23)

This verse does not contain even a drop of baptism as a prerequisite. Which is God's plan, baptism is required, or baptism is not required? God's book, the Bible does not tell me that baptism is required.

Canon 10 supports the teaching of the Catholic church regarding jeopardized salvation through ongoing sin. In the same vein, the Catholic can remain in constant doubt of their eternal relationship with Christ. This doubt leads to increased confession or cleansing, furthered reliance on the forgiveness of sin by God's authorized agent—the priest, and sustained doubt well after death as the soul journeys through purgatory.

"If any one saith, that by the sole remembrance and the faith of the baptism which has been received, all sins committed after baptism are either remitted, or made venial: let him be anathema."

I believe that the Bible tells us to repent of our sin (Matthew 3:2–and yes the kingdom is nearer than ever!). I believe the Bible tells us to confess our sins (1 John 1:9). I also believe that Jesus died once conclusively for all sin. Jesus said

"... It is finished." (John 19:30)

Those three powerful words were the same words used when prisoners were released after serving their sentence. That translation from the Greek means literally "paid in full." Whether Jesus' sacrifice was finished or whether we hear the words "paid in full," the bottom line is the same: All the sins you have committed and will commit were paid for with that one solitary act–His sacrifice. When you accept Christ as your savior, your sins are forgiven; all of them, those past and those yet to be committed. He did it and we cannot undo what God has done. Your salvation is not jeopardized by sin.

The issue of when one is to be baptized is the focus of the next endorsement examined from the Council of Trent. Canon 12 states:

"If any one saith, that no one is to be baptized save at that age at which Christ was baptized, or in the very article of death: let him be anathema."

Christ was baptized at the beginning of His recorded adult ministry at about age 30. Jesus did not teach that there was an appropriate age at which one was to be baptized, but Jesus can be used as the ultimate model for baptism. First, He was not an infant. Second, He never encouraged the baptism of infants. Third, He never taught that anyone may "vouch" for another in baptism, faith, or in salvation. Fourth, when Christ was baptized in the Jordan, "sprinkling" or "pouring" of water was not the technique employed.

Throughout Acts many other baptisms were mentioned. The characteristics above, as portrayed by Christ, remained intact. In all the recorded cases of baptisms in the Bible, the person baptized accepted who Christ was. Christ himself accepted His role fulfilling it to the cross! The traits of Biblical Christian baptism are not exemplified in the baptism of infants: the infant is not a believer; the "sponsor" is not empowered to "vouch" for the child's acceptance of Christ and thereby assure salvation; the infant is a participant void of free will or knowledge of or belief in Christ; and the infant is symbolically sprinkled with water rather than immersed.

## Selected Doctrine On the Sacrament of Confirmation

Confirmation is the last of three Catholic sacraments of initiation including baptism, communion, and confirmation. During confirmation "the laying on of hands" and anointing with oil is received as an acceptance of the responsibility to witness for Christ. The gift of the Holy Spirit is imparted as taught by the Catholic church. The sacrament is usually administered by a bishop and the confirmation candidate has a "sponsor" who assists in the subsequent discipleship of the confirmed.

The book of Acts describes the receipt of the Holy Spirit by those who heard the Word, believed, and prayed [Acts 2:4, 4:31, 8:17]. In the story of Cornelius' household, the "confirmation", facilitated by Peter, preceded "baptism" as described in Acts.

> "While Peter was still speaking these words, the Holy Spirit came on all who heard the message. The circumcised believers who had come with Peter were astonished that the gift of the Holy Spirit had been poured out even on the Gentiles. For they heard them speaking in tongues and praising God.
>
> Then Peter said, "Can anyone keep these people from being baptized with water? They have received the Holy Spirit just as we have." So he ordered that they be baptized in the name of Jesus Christ. Then they asked Peter to stay with them for a few days." (Acts 10:44 - 48)

The gift of the Holy Spirit comes from God. The gift of the Holy Spirit is poured out upon believers. The gift of the Holy Spirit is received according to God's timing. The gift of the Holy Spirit does not come from a man. The gift of the Holy Spirit is not poured out upon non-believers. The gift of the Holy Spirit is not received in accordance with a prescribed pattern of rituals (or ceremonies) as defined by man. The Council of Trent is the definitive authority, as taught by the Catholic church, for confirmation is also found in Canon 1

> "If any one saith, that the confirmation of those who have been baptized is an idle ceremony, and not rather a true and proper sacrament; or that of old it was nothing more than a kind of catechism, whereby they who were near adolescence gave an

account of their faith in the face of the Church: let him be anathema."

So if anyone believes the sacrament of confirmation is a symbolic (idle ceremony) representation of the "laying on of hands" as conducted by the apostles, then this person is accursed by the Catholic church. This judgment undermines the integrity of the Catholic church to administer the gift of the Holy Spirit cursing anyone who questions its authority or dominion to administer God's gifts.

## Selected Doctrines On the Sacrament of Confession

In Mark's Gospel he writes about the paralytic man who sought healing from Jesus. Unfortunately so many people had come to hear Jesus that the paralytic could not even get near Jesus. The four men who were carrying the paralytic cut a hole in the roof of the building and lowered the man.

> "When Jesus saw their faith, he said to the paralytic, 'Son, your sins are forgiven.'
>
> Now some teachers of the law were sitting there, thinking to themselves, 'Why does this fellow talk like that? He's blaspheming! Who can forgive sins but God alone'?" (Mark 2:5 - 7)

Jesus went on to rebuke these teachers. Even the teachers knew that God alone could forgive sins. Jesus told them that He had the authority which they questioned. Canon 6 establishes some of the origins of the sacrament of confession.

> "If any one denieth, either that sacramental confession was instituted, or is necessary to salvation, of divine right; or saith that the manner of confessing secretly to a priest alone, which the Church hath ever observed from the beginning, and doth observe, is alien from the institution and command of Christ, and is a human invention: let him be anathema."

The history of early church does not indicate that confession has been "observed from the beginning." Actually, it took over a thousand years for the Church to accept this doctrine at the Fourth Lateran Council in 1215. This date raises interesting questions regarding those who did not participate in confession prior to the acceptance of this teaching. Are they "damned to hell" too? Were they outside the graces of God? How can any of the early church "saints" be depicted as such (given the curses judged upon them by the Catholic church)?

Each time that I see the words "let him be anathema" I get an uneasy feeling regarding the forgiveness and love Jesus taught, the love and forgiveness that a casual observer might expect to find in "the one true church." This same message was carried forward among believers and was captured by Paul.

> "Be kind and compassionate to one another, forgiving each other, just as in Christ God forgave you." (Ephesians 4:32)

A more exhaustive search of the verb 'confess' discloses its use 17 times in the New Testament. Sixteen of those references encourage us to confess God in the sense of either as our savior and/or before men. The exception appears to be in James.

> And the prayer offered in faith will make the sick person well; the Lord will raise him up. If he has sinned, he will be forgiven. Therefore confess your sins to each other and pray for each other so that you may be healed. The prayer of a righteous man is powerful and effective. (James 5:15 - 16)

Clearly, Jesus' brother tells us to confess to each other and pray for each other. Prayer is 'speaking' to God. When we talk about our sins and take them to the throne of Christ, then we shall know His forgiveness.

As part of the "Lord's Prayer", wherein Jesus taught us what to pray, and while Jesus was praying to our heavenly Father Matthew records

> Forgive us our debts, as we also have forgiven our debtors." (Matthew 6:12)

If Jesus had wanted us to confess only to a priest, and then secretly as well, why did He not articulate those requirements to the apostles? Why did James (in 5:16) write that we should confess to each other and pray for each other?

The need for forgiveness and confession is not unique to the New Testament. In both the Old and New Testaments, God is the one who forgives the sin. In the Old Testament when the people of Israel had sinned and stepped outside God's will, Ezra knew from whom the people needed forgiveness as he implored them:

"Then Ezra the priest stood up and said to them, 'You have been unfaithful; you have married foreign women, adding to Israel's guilt.  Now make confession to the Lord, the God of your fathers, and do his will.  Separate yourselves from the peoples around you and from your foreign wives'."
(Ezra 10:11)

John too reminded us that God forgives our sins as he portrayed:

"If we confess our sins, he is faithful and just and will forgive us our sins and purify us from all unrighteousness."
(1 John 1:9)

John reminds us that our Lord is faithful and just (see Revelation 19:11), that our Lord does forgive us, and that our Lord goes another step further—He purifies us!  Jesus paid it all and Jesus does it all as we allow Him to dominate every aspect of our lives.

According to Scripture, Jesus is the judge, the intercessor, the sole mediator, the sacrifice, and the forgiver.  Let's contrast God's Word with man's word in examining Canon 9 from the Council of Trent regarding the sacrament of confession.

"If any one saith, that the sacramental absolution of the priest is not a judicial act, but a bare ministry of pronouncing and declaring sins to be forgiven to him who confesses; provided only he believe himself to be absolved, or the priest absolve not in earnest, but in joke; or saith, that the confession of the penitent is not required, in order that the priest may be able to absolve him: let him be anathema."

Within this one canon there are several contradictions with Scripture relating to the subjects of judgment, absolution, necessity, and authority.  If you missed some of them you may want to revisit the Scriptures in this section on confession.

In a pamphlet authored by Keith Green entitled "Salvation According to Rome," [3] Dr. Zachello, a former Catholic priest, describes how he came to the realization that he could not forgive sins through the sacrament of confession.

"Where my doubts were really troubling me was inside the confessional box.  People were coming to me, kneeling down in front of me, confessing their sins to me.  And I, with the sign of the cross, was promising that I had the power to forgive their sins. I, a sinner, a man, was taking God's place. It was God's laws they were breaking, not mine. To God, therefore, they must make confession; and to God alone they must pray for forgiveness."

Keith Green's material explores many other issues regarding salvation in the Catholic church. I encourage its review by the interested reader.

Second Vatican Council redefined confession, which now comes in three acceptable varieties. The first, is by the individual person much as described above. The second includes the whole church community with individual confession and absolution as part of the service. The third is general confession and absolution, which can be employed when there are too many penitents. Upon participation in this last form of confession, individuals are expected to confess their "serious sins" privately at a later time. I suspect that "serious sins" is the euphemism for mortal sins as Catholicism attempts to move away from terms like venial and mortal. These new approaches to confession violate the Canons from Trent. Canon 6 is violated because confession is not done secretly and secretly only. Canon 9 is violated because if indeed absolution does occur (as indicated in the Canon) then there would be no need to re-confess "serious sins" at a later time. I suspect that many other contradictions exist; however, I would rather dwell on what is good and pure, that source of truth and light–God's Word.

Finally, Paul describes the Biblical ministry of reconciliation.

"All this is from God, who reconciled us to himself through Christ and gave us the ministry of reconciliation: that God was reconciling the world to himself in Christ, not counting men's sins against them. He has committed to us the message of reconciliation. We are therefore Christ's ambassadors, as though God were making his appeal through us. We implore you on Christ's behalf: Be reconciled to God." (2 Corinthians 5:18 - 20)

| Three things you should know after reading this chapter. |
| --- |

✝   Jesus loves you. God loves you so much that He sent His Son to teach us how to live and most importantly to offer His own life for you.

✝   Jesus seeks a relationship with you. When we break the commandments, we break the commands of God. These actions are called sin and sin interferes in our relationship with God. Sin may keep us from seeing His plan for us or it may prevent us from receiving the blessings He has planned for us. When we sin we need to re-establish our relationship with Him and through Him. Our apology, our repentance, our salvation is through Christ only.

✠ Jesus wants you to love your brothers. When we walk in Christ's light we have fellowship with one another and the blood of His son purifies us. Very similar words are found in First John 1:7. Our path is illuminated by Christ when we follow Him. We cannot follow Him without loving our brothers.

References

[1] John Foxe, <u>Foxe's Christian Martyrs of the World</u>, Barbour and Company, Inc., 1985

[2] Philip Schaff, <u>Creeds of Christendom: With a History and Critical Notes</u>, Harper & Brothers, Franklin Square, 1896

[3] Keith Green, "Salvation According to Rome," distributed by Cultivate Ministries

Other pamphlets from Keith Green:

"What Did Vatican II Really Change?", "The Holy Eucharist", "The Sacrifice of the Mass–What Does It Mean?"

*Paul's advice:*

*be reconciled to God!*

# Chapter 6

## Selected Doctrines on the Mass

W hile growing up in the Catholic church I attended mass weekly. My dad would drive my brother, two sisters, and me to church and then return to pick us up about 45 minutes later. When I entered the Air Force at seventeen, I attended mass often but not always. My perseverance in attending mass diminished until my wife was about to have our first child. Having felt compelled to raise my children as Christians I began to attend mass weekly and have probably missed less than five Sundays in the last ten years. Until the last few years I had no idea what the mass, officially the "Sacrifice of the Mass," was all about.

Many of the doctrines of the mass are documented in the Council of Trent. The "Doctrine on the Sacrifice of the Mass" was penned on September 17, 1562. Still other changes to the mass have occurred as a result of Second Vatican Council. The impact of the Second Vatican Council does not replace or nullify any of the draconian doctrines of Trent. Because of its relevance in the examination of the sacraments and the mass I am repeating Abbott's quotation from The Documents of Vatican II wherein John XXIII describes that the church accepts

"... all the teachings of the Church in its entirety and preciseness, as it still shines forth in the act of the Council of Trent and First Vatican Council ..."

Recently the Catholic church has (in practice) used the phrase the "Celebration of the Mass" rather than the "Sacrifice of the Mass."

While the phraseology has changed and while the mass is now recited in the language of the people, the purpose of the mass has not. The purpose of the mass is to repeat the sacrifice that Christ offered almost 2000 years ago for the atonement of our own sins.

Chapter 2 of the Council (on the Sacrifice of the Mass) makes this point for the interested reader. The quotations in this chapter, from both the Council of Trent and Profession of the Tridentine Faith, are from Philip Schaff's book. [1]

> "Wherefore, not only for the sins, punishments, satisfactions, and other necessities of the faithful who are living, but also for those who are departed in Christ, and who are not as yet fully purified, is it rightly offered, agreeably to a tradition of the apostles."

This quotation implies that the mass is offered for those in Purgatory (not as yet fully purified). The quotation also implies the unrelenting atonement (punishment and satisfactions) that must be endured by the Catholic people. Finally the quotation implies that the tradition began with the apostles although no reference to the Bible is offered. Recognizing these implications explains why the mass is properly called the "Sacrifice." Recognizing these implications explains why the Catholic church would prefer to have the mass thought of as a celebration, but it's not much of either. While the priest prepares for the communion he offers what he believes to be the blood and the body of Christ upon the altar. What most Catholics are not taught is that Christ paid this price in full a long time ago and that no sacrifice that we make can supplement His atonement; He was the Son of God. Who satisfies the needs of the people regarding atonement? Hebrews does a wonderful job of explaining totality and perfection of Christ's atonement.

> "Such a high priest meets our need—one who is holy, blameless, pure, set apart from sinners, exalted above the heavens. Unlike the other high priests, he does not need to offer sacrifices day after day, first for his own sin, and then for the sins of the people. He sacrificed for their sin once for all when he offered himself. For the law appoints as high priests men who are weak; but the oath, which came after the law, appointed the Son, who has been made perfect forever."
> (Hebrews 7:26 - 28)

While the sacrifice of the mass is offered thousands of times each day around the world for the sins of the people, these verses tell us not even God needs to sacrifice or be sacrificed "day after day." These verses tell us that "He sacrificed for their sin once for all when he offered himself." These verses tell us that the Son has been appointed and made perfect forever! Which seems more powerful: the sacrifice offered through the Son of an Almighty God once and forever or the daily (thousands daily) of sacrifices offered by mortal men. Millions of sacrifices offered hourly still would not compare to the act that Jesus completed. Daily offerings were performed in ancient Egyptian temples; but that was a pagan practice and hardly worth emulating. [2]

Read and feel this next passage from Hebrews.

"Nor did he enter heaven to offer himself again and again, the way the high priest enters the Most Holy Place every year with blood that is not his own. Then Christ would have had to suffer many times since the creation of the world. But now he has appeared once for all at the end of the ages to do away with sin by the sacrifice of himself." (Hebrews 9:25 - 26)

The key points reinforced in this passage from Hebrews teach us that He did not need to be offered repeatedly; He did not need to suffer many times; He only had to appear once; and He alone and all sufficiently stole the penalty of death from sin with His sacrifice. Hebrews also describes the effectiveness of man's sacrifices

"Day after day every priest stands and performs his religious duties; again and again he offers the same sacrifices, which can never take away sins." (Hebrews 10:11)

Canon 2 raises the issues of transubstantiation and while I do not agree with this Catholic doctrine I believe it is the intent (not the substance, which is still another issue) of what is offered during communion, which is the issue. I believe the aforementioned reference by Mr. Green adequately addresses the following Canon.

"If any one saith, that by those words, 'do this for the commemoration of me', Christ did not institute the apostles priests; or, did not ordain that they and other priests should offer his own body and blood: let him be anathema."

Canon 3 depicts the "sacrifice" of the mass as well as its purpose, which is for the propitiation of sin. Its content is also addressed with the verses from Hebrews.

> "If any one saith, that the sacrifice of the mass is only a sacrifice of praise and thanksgiving; or, that it is a bare commemoration of the sacrifice consummated on the cross, but not a propitiatory sacrifice; or, that it profits him only who receives; and that it ought not be offered for the living and the dead for sin, pains, satisfactions, and other necessities: let him be anathema."

Many Bible believing Christians understand that because Christ offered His life on the cross, any other attempted sacrifice would be a mere feeble imitation. Worse yet, any other sacrifice is a rejection of the sacrifice Christ paid for us all–once and for all and a denial of faith in the act He performed. It appears Canon 4 was written to address this belief.

> "If any one saith, that, by the sacrifice of the mass, a blasphemy is cast upon the most holy sacrifice of Christ consummated on the cross; or, that it is thereby derogated from: let him be anathema."

Pius IV, writing during the same times as the Council of Trent in the Profession of the Tridentine Faith, Article 6 affirmed this teaching of the purpose of the sacrifice of the mass.

> "I profess, likewise, that in the mass there is offered to God a true, proper, and propitiatory sacrifice for the living and the dead; ..."

Of course since Second Vatican Council, the Catholic church has attempted to soften some of its harsher stances. In some cases however, this softening has tended to remove the clarity of the purpose of the mass and accompanying sacraments. Ernest Falardeau offered the following four quotations in "The Eucharist and forgiveness of sins" [3].

> "We usually think of the Sacrament of Reconciliation as the Sacrament 'for the forgiveness of sins'. But the Eucharist is also a sacrament of forgiveness."

> "Usually I think of Christ's death on the cross "for the forgiveness of sins" before I think of a sacrament. If I focus on

my participation in a ceremonial rite rather than His sacrifice
then my focus is on the wrong event."

"Forgiveness of sins begins at Baptism."

Forgiveness does indeed begin with baptism and baptism with
repentance. Matthew, Mark, and Luke describe John the Baptist; his
message and his work.

"Confessing their sins, they were baptized by him in the
Jordan River." (Matthew 3:6)

"And so John came, baptizing in the desert region and
preaching a baptism of repentance for the forgiveness of sins."
(Mark 1:4)

"He went into all the country around the Jordan, preaching a
baptism of repentance for the forgiveness of sins." (Luke 3:3)

Please note however, that an infant cannot confess their sins; they have
no concept of sin. Without the concept of sin there can be no desire to
repent. Repentance is necessary for forgiveness. Forgiveness is made
reality in the life of the believer when Christ is accepted as a personal
savior.

"The Eucharist is given to us 'for the remission of sins which
we daily commit'. The words of Institution, in particular over
the cup, emphasize that the blood of Christ is/was "poured
out" for the remission of sins."

Clearly though, Falardeau reinforces the primary purpose of the mass—
the ongoing remission of sin. The overview of the verses in Hebrews is
not consistent with the continuous "pouring out" of blood. While I do
not intend to revisit those critical points, Falardeau's article documents
that Christ's single act and all sufficient sacrifice is not enough for our
sins; rather, that only through the traditions of man can an adequate
sacrifice be offered. Additionally, Christ's sacrifice is supplemented
daily for our daily sins and not just once but thousands of times
throughout the world.

## Masses in Honor of the "Saints"

Sometimes the church offers masses in honor of "saints," although Christ
is still sacrificed in these masses, too. In the Council's 22nd session,
Chapter 3 are the words:

"And although the Church has been accustomed at times to celebrate certain masses in honor and memory of the saints; not therefore, however, doth she teach that sacrifice is offered unto them, but unto God alone, who crowned them; whence neither is the priest wont to say, ' I offer sacrifice to thee, Peter or Paul; but, giving thanks to God for their victories, he implores their patronage, that they may vouchsafe to intercede for us in heaven, whose memory we celebrate upon earth."

Compare this teaching of intercession with the story of the rich man and Lazarus taught by Jesus and captured by Luke.

"There was a rich man who was dressed in purple and fine linen and lived in luxury every day. At his gate was laid a beggar named Lazarus, covered with sores and longing to eat what fell from the rich man's table. Even the dogs came and licked his sores.

The time came when the beggar died and the angels carried him to Abraham's side. The rich man also died and was buried. In hell, where he was in torment, he looked up and saw Abraham far away, with Lazarus by his side. So he called to him, 'Father Abraham, have pity on me and send Lazarus to dip the tip of his finger in the water and cool my tongue, because I am in agony in this fire.'

But Abraham replied, 'Son, remember that in your lifetime you received your good things, while Lazarus received bad things, but now he is comforted here and you are in agony. And besides all this, between us and you a great chasm has been fixed, so that those who want to go from here to you cannot, nor can anyone cross over from there to us.'

He answered, 'Then I beg you, father, send Lazarus to my father's house, for I have five brothers. Let him warn them, so that they will not also come to this place of torment.'

Abraham replied, 'They have Moses and the Prophets; let them listen to them.'

'No, father Abraham,' he said, 'but if someone from the dead goes to them, they will repent.'

He said to him, 'If they do not listen to Moses and the
Prophets, they will not be convinced even if someone rises
from the dead'." (Luke 16:19 - 31)

Where did the beggar go? Where did the rich man go? Where was
purgatory? How was hell described? To whom did the rich man call
out? Could anyone cross from either side? How many sides were
there? What did the rich man request for his brothers? What did
Abraham reply? To whom should the brothers listen? Was the
negotiation in verse 30 effective? What was the effectiveness of the
rich man's plea bargain? Was Abraham in any position to barter for the
rich man? Who alone can negotiate on our behalf before the Father?
How many times is a man judged?

In February of 1992 in the People of God Catholic newspaper, was this
insight on praying to saints. [4]

"Saints are not worshipped or adored. Only God is adored.
But saints are venerated as models inspiring us to imitate their
holiness ... We ask saints to pray for us."

So the doctrine of intercession, through someone or something other
than God, remains a very active part of Catholic teaching today.
However, you will not find the endorsement of any such praying to the
dead (worse yet as intercessors) in the Bible. We are commanded not
even to contact the dead.

Pius IV in Article 8 of the Profession of the Tridentine Faith, certified
the reason for the Catholic church's honoring of the dead during the
times of the Council of Trent.

"I firmly hold that there is a purgatory, and that the souls
therein detained are helped by the suffrages of the faithful.
Likewise, that the saints reigning with Christ are to be honored
and invoked, and that they offer up prayers to God for us, and
that their relics are to be had in veneration."

From Pius' endorsements, purgatory is reinforced, praying to and
invoking (as in spirits) saints is sanctioned, and in direct contradiction
to God's laws, treating objects as worthy of adoration. The children of
Israel were directed to avoid idolatry and the Lord made it abundantly
clear in Deuteronomy what was to be avoided

"so that you do not become corrupt and make for yourselves an
idol, an image of any shape, whether formed like a man or a

woman, or like any animal on earth of any bird that flies in the air, or like any creature that moves along the ground or any fish in the waters below." (Deuteronomy 4:16 - 19)

As recorded in Deuteronomy, when Moses received the Ten Commandments he was told:

"You shall not make for yourself an idol in the form of anything in heaven above or on the earth beneath or in the waters below. You shall not bow down to them or worship them; for I, the Lord your God, am a jealous God, punishing the children for the sin of the fathers to the third and fourth generation of those who hate me, but showing love to a thousand generations of those who love me and keep my commandments." (Deuteronomy 5:8 - 10)

The above verses appear to cover all man-made idols of worship including: statues, medals, beads, windows, icons, and scapulars. The specific warnings regarding bowing down and worship are clear. God gives us the reason–He wants our undivided attention and focus on the true source of life and goodness–Him!

A prayer card distributed by the Dominican Fathers related to the Shrine of St. Jude Thaddeus purports

"I promise you, O blessed JUDE, to be ever mindful of this great favor, and I will never cease to honor you as my special and powerful patron and do all in my power to encourage devotion to you."

As Christians our devotion is to Christ. We should never cease to honor Christ all the days of our lives. If there is any favor for which we ought to be ever mindful, it is the sacrifice Jesus provided for each of us. If we love the Lord with all our hearts, soul, and strength, from where do we sustain additional "power" to encourage devotion to anything other than Christ himself? Let us not divide our attention. Let us not lose our focus. In Psalm 34:1 David wrote how he would extol the Lord at all times, with His praise continually on his lips.

## Only the Catholic Church Understands Things of a Divine Nature

This next excerpt seems to insult anyone, Catholic or non-Catholic, for attempting to know God personally and growing in Him through His Word as guided by the Holy Spirit.  Instead, this pronouncement places everyone under the interpretation of the Catholic church.  The quotation is found in Chapter 5 (again from the Council of Trent and its section on the sacrifice of the mass).

"And whereas such is the nature of man, that, without external helps, he can not easily be raised to the meditation of divine things; therefore has holy Mother Church instituted certain rites, to wit, that certain things be pronounced in the mass in a low, and others in a louder tone.  She has likewise employed ceremonies, such as mystic benedictions, lights, incense, vestments, and many other things of this kind, derived from an apostolical discipline and tradition, ..."

The words know, knowest, knoweth, knowing, knowledge, and known are found approximately 1450 times in the Bible.  Apparently there's a whole lot more that Christ wanted us to know than the Catholic church is conceding.  Hebrews reassures:

"No longer will a man teach his neighbor, or a man his brother, saying, Know the Lord, because they will all know me, from the least of them to the greatest."  (Hebrews 8:11)

Examine for yourself the following verses from First John to see if the language is ambiguous or in any way needs interpretation.

"We know that we have come to know him if we obey his commands."  (1 John 2:3)

"But you have an anointing from the Holy One, and all of you know the truth.  I do not write to you because you do not know the truth, but because you do know it and because no lie comes from the truth."  (1 John 2:20 - 21)

"But whoever hates his brother is in the darkness and walks around in the darkness; he does not know where he is going, because the darkness has blinded him."  (1 John 2:11)

"Dear friends, now we are children of God, and what we will be has not yet been made known.  But we know that when he

appears, we shall be like him, for we shall see him as he is."
(1 John 3:2)

"This is how we know who the children of God are and who
the children of the devil are: Anyone who does not do what is
right is not a child of God; nor is anyone who does not love his
brother." (1 John 3:10)

"I write these things to you who believe in the name of the
Son of God so that you may know that you have eternal life."
(1 John 5:13)

I have not included the other 1440 plus verses but God gave you a mind
with which to know Him. James tells us that God will provide us
generously with wisdom if we ask Him for it (James 1:5). We cannot
stand before God and tell Him He left us unequipped or unreached. He
has already provided for us in every way.

This teaching of the Catholic church was also confirmed by Pius IV in
the "Profession of the Tridentine Faith", Article 3. In this article the
pope limits his own infallible understanding as it pertains to the
Scriptures.

"I also admit the holy Scriptures, according to that sense
which our holy mother Church has held and does hold, to
which it belongs to judge of the true sense and interpretation
of the Scriptures; neither will I ever take and interpret them
otherwise than according to the unanimous consent of the
Fathers."

The Sacrifice of the Mass, the repeated sacrificing of Christ on the
altar, the unrelenting spilling of His blood, is not consistent with the
teachings found in the book of Hebrews. I do appreciate the intended
honor that is repeatedly offered by the Catholic church to Jesus for His
sacrifice for my sins. The repetition of His sacrifice, a once and for all
event, may evidence a lack of faith in His singular and all sufficient
atonement.

As we keep our eyes and focus on the Creator, we will seek no other
presence, guidance, or intercession from any lesser entity. For there is
only one God, and He being all knowing, all powerful, and always
present, can certainly handle my needs.

No person and no institution will win the confidence I have in God to
provide for and teach me. Therefore, no person and no institution will

disrupt my personal relationship with Christ; for matters of unprecedented importance, I also must entrust to Him alone and directly.

| Three things you should know after reading this chapter. |

✞ Jesus loves you. Jesus already died for your sins. You need to worship the Son of God, not to sacrifice the Son of God. Christ has risen and is preparing a place for you.

✞ Jesus seeks a relationship with you. You can know that you have a relationship with Him that cannot be replaced by performing rituals and traditions in His honor. Your relationship with Him comes from Him and not through others.

✞ Jesus wants you to love your brothers. Share Christ's one-to-one relationship with those you come into contact with today. When you share God, you share love, for God is love. And He commanded us to love.

References

[1] Philip Schaff, <u>Creeds of Christendom: With a History and Critical Notes</u>, Harper & Brothers, Franklin Square, 1896

[2] Geoffrey Parrinder, <u>World Religions From Ancient History to the Present</u>, Facts On File Publications, 1983

[3] Ernest Falardeau, "The Eucharist and forgiveness of sins," <u>People of God</u>, September, 1990

[4] Edward McCarthy, "Renewing Our Faith—Part Three," <u>People of God</u>, February 1992

> *Speaking from Scripture,*
>
> *Purgatory is an open and closed case.*
>
> *If you open the Word, you will not find it.*
>
> *Case closed!*

# Chapter 7

## The Good News from Second Vatican Council (Sounds a Lot Like the Bad News from Earlier Councils)

W hile compiling this book I must admit I read more Catholic literature than at anytime previously in my life. By exploring the Scripture for the truth for the past nine years, I searched in earnest to find the message from Catholicism was missing–that one overlooked detail, the one piece of knowledge that made it all somehow fit together. I read about former evangelicals who turned Catholic (yes evangelicals, there is at least one.) I attempted to read the works of authors that appeared to be "scholarly" in their explanations of Catholicism. I also became more aware of former Catholic priests who left the Catholic church. The most apparent divergences came in a pair. First, those who sided with the "majesty of the mass" and the formality of the rites appeared to be placing their trust in tradition. Those who sided with the sufficiency of the Bible appeared to be placing their trust in the faithfulness of the Word. Second, typically the proponents and defendants of Catholicism continue to blame and degrade the Protestant movement. Typically, the proponents and defendants of Christianity perceived Satan as the source of many of the difficulties in reconciling ecumenical differences.

Even since the advent of Second Vatican Council, the lack of ecumenicalism in words and practice by Catholics towards Protestants, is widely evident. Dear Catholics, I think you are missing the point just as much as the participants at Trent missed the issues in the days of the reformation.  Protestants are not Protestants for the sake of standing against the Catholic church.  Many of the labeled "Protestants" are believers primarily interested in their relationship with Jesus Christ; they are Christians not Protestants.  Unceasing animosity towards "separated brethren" (translation–anyone outside the Catholic church) is detestable and that applies equally regardless of which direction the attacks flow. Allow me to provide you with just a few examples of the assaults perpetrated recently.

To those Christians who maintain the inerrancy of Scripture, Second Vatican Council affirmed

> "Scripture must be acknowledged as teaching firmly,
> faithfully, and without error that truth which God wanted put
> into the sacred writing for the sake of our salvation."

Why is the qualification "without error" only as it pertains to salvation accentuated?  Is not Scripture the perfect truth for how to treat one another?  Is it not the source of perfect truth for living as a Christian community?  Second Vatican Council perpetuated the issue of inerrancy, sending clear indications the Catholic church was unwilling to soften the teachings of tradition; from wherein, the church admittedly obtains its authority.  Such a loosely worded statement does little to explain Second Timothy 3:16 wherein we are reminded that all Scripture comes from God.  While Second Vatican Council did not directly confirm its two sources of truth (Scripture and its tradition) it did proclaim

> "It is not Scripture alone that the Church draws her certainty
> about everything which has been revealed."

No doubt that part of the mood on inerrancy stemmed from a belief that mainline Protestants were not upholding inerrancy.  Again the Catholic church continues to disguise its own positions by comparing itself with what it perceives to be the endorsements of the Protestant movement. Unfortunately the measuring rod is, as it always has been, Scripture. Unfortunately the Catholic church continues to segregate (or perhaps assume integration with the Christian community) between Catholics and Protestants.  Unfortunately, the Catholic church has not conducted its research if it believes "mainline Protestants" are not upholding the issue of inerrancy.

## The Crusades Continue (In Verbal Form)

This section presents just a few writings, many of which were collected before the notion of developing a book had occurred. These materials were collected because the words and themes were quite contrary to what I then believed to be the core and essential teachings of the Bible. Those words and themes frequently contradict the core and essential teachings of the Bible. The veracities of those beliefs in the accuracy of the Scriptures are documented throughout the various chapters of this book.

Six quotations that were received in late 1991 and early 1992 as parts of a church newsletter [1] are examined. The material is therefore relatively recently endorsed. It was distributed locally yet its source is much more widely disseminated. It was written about a council convened almost 30 years ago. Yet it demonstrates the length and the strength of the reins of the papacy. It also yields some very questionable language that might be a concern to people regardless of denominational affiliation. For instance this first quotation illustrates the willingness of the Catholic church to adopt the vernacular of the day in an attempt to "reach out and touch" in a universal fashion.

1.  The church must keep pace with the times and enter fully into the new age now being born.

This interesting wording is consistent with popular "new age" thinking. It implies the church needs to change, adapt, or accelerate its perspectives to prepare for a new age. Apparently the Catholic church has taken this precept seriously; for the past 1500 years or so. Christ tells us in Matthew 24, Mark 13, and Luke 21 to beware of the signs of the "end of the age" not the signs of a "new age." The new age doctrines are human-centric, and under closer scrutiny, egocentric. They are harmonious with end times' doctrines including the falling away, or apostasy, from Christ-centered worship. God's Word stands firm against the test of time. God's Word sets the pace; a pace too often abandoned. Directly tied to the new age egocentric perspective is the next quotation.

2.  The Church is an institution of human beings on earth.

Perhaps the Catholic church has become an institution of human-beings on earth. To many others, the church is a place of adoration and worship. Yet the Biblical use of the word "church" is the body of believers, the body of Christ as portrayed in Colossians.

> "And he is the head of the body, the church, he is the beginning and the firstborn from among the dead, so that in everything he might have the supremacy." (Colossians 1:18)

> "Now I rejoice in what was suffered for you, and I fill up in my flesh what is still lacking in regard to Christ's afflictions, for the sake of his body, which is the church." (Colossians 1:24)

This human-centric delusion continues when leaders of the Catholic church are described as images of Christ.

3.    Bishops and Pastor are, in their own right, "Vicars of Christ."

Ironically, it is the Protestants who are accused of acting as their own popes as portrayed by Mr. Davies [2]. The phrase "Vicar of Christ" is discussed in the third chapter of this book with other issues concerning the papacy. In the sight of the Catholic church, these offices do serve as the substitutes of Christ here on earth. The above quotation tacitly accepts that thousands of "substitutes" are now administering on behalf of the Catholic church. We need to recall that Christ alone is head of the true Church–His Church. We also need to recognize that He alone is God and there's but one and one alone! Recognizing that the Church is His Body, then the validity of the next quotation seems suspect.

4.    In and from such churches comes into being the one and only Catholic Church.

We know the word "Catholic" does not appear in Scripture. We know therefore, there is no Biblical revelation concerning the above assertion. We also know from history that the word "Catholic" was not adopted by the early church communities until hundreds of years after Christ rose from the dead. Christ's message of loving Him and each other is found throughout the Bible. These actions may result in the ecumenical unity espoused in a one and only church. Even in Revelation 2 and 3 seven "churches" are addressed. Is the following excerpt reflective of the love He commanded us to have?

5.    We must have a reverence for the heritage of other Christian churches. We must overcome hatred and suspicion and be open to appreciate all sound values in other forms of Christianity.

On the surface, these words sound rather comforting. The meaning however, remains elusive. The "reverence" is for the "heritage" not necessarily its foundation in Biblical teaching. The intent is to "appreciate" rather than to accept. Note the openness and appreciation will be for "sound values." Typically, these "sound values" are those endorsed by Catholic teaching. The Catholic church has stated its positions on numerous occasions in its various councils. At times the packaging of the wording is softened, such as at Vatican Council II; but, the message has been and continues to be the same. More than one church claims to be the one and only true church. The Catholic position on this teaching is not unique; yet, its non-uniqueness does not afford the teachings any additional palatability.

6.  We can recognize elements of truth and goodness in all great religions, but insisted on the God-given uniqueness of the church of Christ.

Historically, documents released by the Catholic church indicate its uniqueness and its apostolic receivership. If we examine this statement in a wider context (which I do not believe is its intended meaning), Christianity as a whole needs to insist on the uniqueness of churches adhering to the Word, to churches where love flows abundantly, and to churches that have Christ as its central figure and lone object of adoration. Instead, Second Vatican Council reasserts its position as "the church" guided by the spirit as supported by these words from the Council.

> The Spirit guides the Church into the fullness of truth and gives her a unity of fellowship and service.

Considering the anathemas from the Council of Trent, the above words are reassuring that both a change of heart and perhaps a change of doctrine are possibilities if not actualities. The next "proof" then is the test of the actions accompany the words. John reminds us:

> "Dear children, let us not love with words and tongue but with actions and in the truth." (1 John 3:18)

While not directly relevant to our salvation, these words teach us the foundation of integrity. So while Second Vatican Council may not consider these words to be inerrant, I accept them as true. Let's examine a few instances of the ecumenical spirit of the Catholic church since Second Vatican Council. Consider the following examples in light of the stated guidance for "unity of fellowship and service."

The <u>People of God</u> is an award winning Catholic circular.  In May of 1992, in an article describing a Mexican diocese that was formed as counter to Protestant influence in Mexico, the following words were found [3].

> The new Diocese of Tlapa was established to counteract the influence of Protestantism in the impoverished and mountainous southwestern Mexico region.  Expressing concern over the spread of Protestant churches in the area, Mexican church leaders had petitioned the Vatican to create the new see.  "The sects are like flies," the apostolic delegate to Mexico, Archbishop Girolamo Prigione, was quoted as saying ... "They may bother us, but they will never bring the Catholic Church down."

I think you will agree that such language can hardly be interpreted as intended to do good; yet, I suspect that the outburst of "flies" in Mexico is an attempt to fill a void and bring the people a personal knowledge and relationship with Jesus Christ.

In the article Interchurch families celebrating baptism [4] Ernest Falardeau writes

> One important principle rediscovered at the Second Vatican Council is that the Church is a communion.  All those baptized and believe in Jesus Christ as Son of God and Savior are part of that communion of faith.

Note that the following careful wording comes very close to sounding as if all those who are in "communion" are also saved.  This proximity is deceptive.  Examine the following simple four-step argument:

1.  The pope is infallible, his teachings are irreversible.

2.  The Council of Trent asserts that no one can be saved outside the Catholic church.

3.  Pius IV, a pope, endorsed all the declarations from the Council of Trent in the Profession of the Tridentine Faith, Article 5, long after the Council.

    > "I embrace and receive all and every one of the things which have been defined and declared in the holy Council of Trent concerning original sin and justification."

4.    Therefore, it is irreversible doctrine of the Catholic church to portray anyone outside the Catholic church as saved!

Pius went one step further in helping to illustrate this point. In Article 12 of the same document he writes

> "I do, at this present, freely profess and truly hold this true Catholic faith, without which no one can be saved; ..."

Michael Parise addresses several doctrinal differences from the Catholic perspective in a tract by the name of "Are We the One True Church?" [5]   As a post Second Vatican Council work, examine the careful wording and the conclusion that those outside the Catholic church are still "not saved."

> "The Catholic Church recognizes that many of these Protestant communions have preserved essential elements of Christ's true Church.   To the degree that Protestant communions preserve and promote true elements of Christ's Church, they are related to Roman Catholics, fellow disciples on the road to salvation."

Is the writing of Parise an example of the "unity" aspired by the Second Vatican Council or is it really more reflective of the traditional teachings of the Catholic church?   Are these carefully phrased words any less condemning than the original curses from the Council of Trent? In the article "Lutheran-Catholic dialogue recognizes authentic Marian devotion is not idolatrous" [6] Catholics proclaim

> "That in a close but still incomplete fellowship, Lutherans, focusing on Christ the one mediator, as set forth in Scripture, would not be obliged to invoke the saints or affirm the two Marian dogmas ..."

More recently, others have reflected back to the period just preceding the Council of Trent.   In Peter's Kingdom [7], speaking of Clement VII, the Jerrold Packard notes

> "... he might have taken much of the wind out of the Protestants' sails before they had a chance to consolidate their schism; when he didn't, the opportunity was lost forever."

Packard's language portrays a lost opportunity (on the part of the Catholic church) by not thwarting the Protestant movement.   By Clement VII's reign however, the papacy had already committed such heinous acts that it was obvious the Catholic church had abandoned its own people.   Just a few years thereafter, the Council of Trent intentionally created what still appears to be an irreconcilable set of distinguishing doctrines with over 100 accompanying accurses hurled at dissenters.   Today, very few Catholics are unaware that many of those curses apply equally to their own ranks–yes even after Vatican II.

Thomas Bokenkotter's <u>Essential Catholicism</u> [8], affirms the careful wording of the church regarding the doctrine of salvation for non-Catholics (parenthetical inclusion mine).

> "The (Second Vatican) council recognized all those Christians who dwell outside the boundaries but share in many of the blessings of the Gospel, ... They, too, receive the gifts and graces of the Holy Spirit and by him are in some real way joined with 'us'."

How is it that believers in the risen Christ share in the blessings of the Gospel while outside the boundaries of what, the doctrines of the Catholic church?   What is this "real way" in which we are enjoined? What is the Scriptural reference for this theology?

Still another camp challenges Vatican II.   This camp emanates from a band of conservatives within the Catholic church that demonstrate the harm to the Catholic church as a result of the Council.   Michael Davies documents many of these concerns in <u>Pope John's Council</u> [2].   Some of the themes in Davies' book include:

• self-destruction within the Catholic church since the Council

• the notion that each Protestant (does Davies mean believer in Christ) is a Pope unto themselves

• that no positive statements can be made about Protestantism

• that Protestant acceptance of some Council doctrines should in itself be a serious concern to Rome

• the infiltration of Masons into the Catholic church and its hierarchy

• massive declines in attendance at mass in several European countries including Italy, as well as the US.

• similar declines in calls to the priesthood in most of the same countries

• tremendous declines in baptisms in England, Wales, and the US.

Davies' work is very well written and supported. His numbers come directly from Catholic publications. Here follows the twist. I am uncomfortably aware that in the end times a great apostasy will occur within the body of Christ; that is, more will fall away from His teachings in those last days. Does Davies research indicate such an apostasy? I believe not, if those former Catholics are living in Christ as part of another congregation. Is this mass "exodus" from the Catholic church a "final call" before the sounding of the trumpet that directly precedes Christ's return? A proliferation of cults and a quick scan of your local paper or evening news will confirm that the apostasy is accelerating, it is alive and well.

Supporting evidence for a decline in the power of the church of Rome can be found in other countries and continents. In the pope's own homeland, attendance within the Catholic community has dropped from 75 percent participation to just 15 percent. These figures were reported in a newsletter in March of 1992 published by Thru the Bible Radio. Whether it's South America and Brazil (see the Chapter 3) or Eurasia and Poland, more folks are being turned off by and tuned out from the Catholic church. For them, finding the truth is an essence of time. Many former Catholics consider the Catholic church to be "idolatrous," weak in Scriptural exegesis, or have left Catholicism as a result of "bad experiences with a priest." [9]

In the state of Hawaii, "holy days of obligation" are being reduced to two: Christmas and the Immaculate Conception [10]. Members of the Catholic community in Hawaii are being asked to view these two remaining days as "holy days of celebration." The reaction of Rome to this change and its impact on other Catholic communities deserves watching (from an arm's length distance).

Our role needs to be to counteract the apostasy that already began (1 John 2:19, and 4:3) and will eclipse. Our role is to offer God's plan to every possible contact prior to the fulfillment of the "falling away." This quest serves to remind me how much work I have remaining to do as well.

I remember searching for good Christian couples who might serve as godparents for our son Joshua some ten years ago. I remember conversing with the couple that eventually accepted that responsibility and how they reminded me of my responsibilities to raise Joshua.

Discussion ensued revolving around Catholic doctrine and Biblical teaching; in essence, salvation in accordance with Catholicism versus salvation in accordance with Scripture. As both sets of our families grew and grew up we have spent less time together but I appreciate their initial commitment to Joshua's maturity as a Christian.

On Good Friday in 1992 I was challenged by Joshua's godmother scorning that I should not be eating meat that day. Actually I was eating turkey (although I do not know if turkey is regarded by the Catholic church as a meat.) I responded that "we'll need to talk about that some time." The conversation reminded me of what a poor job I had been doing of sharing my faith, especially with strong Catholics like her and her husband. The conversation reminded me that I had left the Catholic church years earlier but that we were not close enough to discuss matters of utmost importance. The conversation reminded me that I was the problem; that I should be sharing more in verbal form not just written. I wondered what other doctrines she might be practicing that hindered rather than enhanced her relationship with God. I am grateful that she was bold enough to speak to me that day. I pray for the wisdom to approach her and discuss the meaning of Colossians 2:16.

As Christians, our missionary efforts can be next door, across the street, or thousands of miles from "home." Christians everywhere have an opportunity to reach literally millions in the former Soviet Union. A graphic in the People of God newspaper, copyrighted in 1991 by CNS (Catholic News Service), notes the rise in the number of Soviet Catholic, Russian Orthodox, and other non-Catholic churches. In recent years, the number of all listed churches rose.

I wonder if the appeal of Christ's presence to the Soviet people will someday reflect a sign in front of Saint Dominic Savio in Affton, Missouri, which read "Come early & get a back seat"! We need to be better witnesses for getting close to the Father than is reflected in the light-hearted sign. If you do not feel like you both need and want to get closer to God, you are either in rebellion against God or worshiping in the wrong place. I really look forward to my Sunday services.

Our joy in Christ is not restricted to Sunday. Bible studies, Christian television and radio, prayer partnerships, choirs, ministries outside of church, readings, fellowship, and walking in the Spirit supplement the Christian walk each and every day. Praying for the struggles of others and keeping God first and in focus ease the walk here. My time with

Him is exciting.  His affirmations are overwhelming.  This attitude helps to complete our joy in Christ.

The Catholic church feels challenged by its continued teachings of "tradition" equality with Scripture.  The following quotations are extracted from the article The Fundamentalist Challenge published in the <u>Catholic Update</u> written by Raymond E. Brown [11].  The first quotation evidences the lack of confidence of the Holy Spirit as co-author of the Bible.

> "It [fundamentalism] does not recognize that every word in the Bible, even though inspired by God, has been written by human beings who had limitations."

Imagine the limits of the first writer of the Scriptures–Moses.  He was so limited that through the power of God he sent ten plagues upon the nation of Egypt, performed miracles in their sight, and parted the Red Sea so that the children of Israel crossed on dry land.  Most of Moses' life appeared to be beyond the expected boundaries of human limitations.  Was David bound by human limitations even as a young boy?  Was Daniel depicted as limited when he "served time" in the lion's den?  Were the original apostles and later Paul hindered by the notion of limitations when they performed miracles of raising the dead and healing?  Following the author Brown's logic then, must we also dismiss the other writings of Scripture that appear beyond the capabilities of the physical man?  What then would remain of God's Holy Word?  This rationale continues in the next quotation.

> "One must understand that only human beings speak words. Therefore the very valid description of the Bible as 'God's word' has both the divine element ('God's') and the human ('word'). "

Again, let's test this statement in contrast to Scripture.  God spoke first to Adam and Eve.  He spoke to Moses directly on numerous occasions. God spoke to the prophets.  Jesus, who was and is God, spoke in words that were recorded in Greek.  The Lord spoke to Paul.  All of these instances of God's verbal expression were delivered with words.  While God made us in His image, God is spirit.  Brown's belief that only "human beings speak words" does not align with Scripture (see Revelation 19:9 as one example).  Yet, the article continues stating "The Roman Catholic Church considers itself a biblical Church", which is correct to the extent that Scripture concurs with its teachings;

otherwise, Fundamentalists are too cautious remaining within strict Biblical conformance.

Brown continues by offering responses to ten issues Catholics may not find themselves equipped to deal with when discussing the Bible with "fundamentalists." In offering an explanation for praying to saints he writes

> "Roman Catholicism has recognized the intercession of the saints. That is part of its understanding of the biblical injunction that we must pray for one another."

Since Brown attempts to offer a strong argument for the "human limitations" of the writers of the Bible, I am surprised he would then rely upon the "humanly limited" to interpret the Bible using words and meanings that do not exist in Scripture. Ephesians 6:18 does remind us to pray for one another. Please note the word "for" and not "to" which changes the entire meaning of the text. This slight twist of words, a complete replacement of the Word with tradition, is a frequently used tactic to support non-Biblical Catholic teaching.

Brown explains the leadership of the pope as

> "an overseer through whom Christ supplies guidance to the whole Church, keeping it in the truth of the gospel."

Brown does not explain the personal relationship man is to have with His Savior; instead deflecting the relationship through the pope as another layer of intercession. Shortly thereafter in defense of the doctrines of Mary's Immaculate Conception and Assumption, Brown admits that these teachings "are not found in the New Testament." Further, these doctrines are not found in the Old Testament or anywhere in Scripture yet Brown ascribes the guidance and truth of the gospel to the pope who endorses these doctrines. Brown suggests that a potential problem associated with the reading of the Bible might be that "Individuals from their Bible reading may come to radical conclusions. This has indeed happened in the course of history." Luke encourages his readers in Acts 17:11 that they should search the Scripture daily to see if what they are being taught (or hear) is true. So once again, the Scripture is the yardstick according to Luke. Brown closes with this sentence.

> "It [the Catholic church] resists the use of biblical interpretation to support scientific or historical statements that

lay beyond the competency of the biblical authors in their times."

In closing Brown completes his subtle attack on the writers of the Scripture by questioning their competency in regard to "matters of fact." Rather, the Catholic church would suggest, as it has historically, that it alone is the authority for interpreting Scripture. Brown makes this point self-evident in his writing.

In the spring of 1990, the People of God newspaper included an article entitled "The Threat of Fundamentalism" [12]. Why a belief centered in the Word of God, would be considered threatening to any self-proclaimed Bible-believing Christian denomination, escapes my thinking. In this article, the editor questions the motive of those who are drawn into fundamentalist circles while again asserting the Biblical soundness of the Catholic doctrine.

"The Fundamentalists do not draw people through union of mind or will, that is, through deeper insight into the meaning of the Scriptures, or through commitment to higher ideals, than what we have as Catholics. They draw people through an experience of emotions: the feeling of warmth and oneness with others in the expression of faith and love for Jesus. But I might point out that since true union of heart is impossible without union of mind and will, those who want to keep experiencing this emotional unity must sooner or later accept fundamentalist doctrine and commit themselves to the rules, the goals, and ideals of whatever group to which they are attached."

I believe the attraction to Fundamentalists that is overlooked by the author is the union we share as children of God; as co-heirs through His atonement. The "feeling of warmth and oneness with others" is only part of the experience missing from the Catholic church. As evidenced earlier through its doctrines and teachings, the Catholic church has alienated both its members and other "separated brethren." Another part of the missing experience is the validity of the Bible and accuracy of its writers. I agree with the closing of this quotation. At some point we need to commit ourselves to the ideals of fellow worshippers. What better an ideal to commit ourselves to than the truth of Scripture and not the traditions passed along between generations? If being close to the Scriptures and seeking a one-on-one relationship with the Father through His Son Jesus Christ is a threat to the Catholic church, then fundamentally speaking, it is the Catholic church, which is the true threat to its own membership.

The preceding examples serve to highlight many of the current sentiments and reactions of Catholics towards non-Catholic Christian denominations. Pope John Paul II has offered guidelines for criticism to be applied within the Catholic church. The guidelines seem quite constructive and positive imploring no bitterness, non-offensiveness, nor damage to "the honor of persons and groups." Catholic church officials then determine whether such criticisms are the result of genuine gifts which "produce joy and peace". Contrary to earlier "infallible" popes and their papal campaigns that exterminated groups within the Catholic church, (see Chapter 3), John Paul states that "the Church has always recognized the value of charisms among all its members." [13]   While John Paul's guidelines for criticism are useful, perhaps they could be extended beyond the boundaries of the Catholic church and also be applied to the tones used by the Catholic church towards what it describes still as "separated brethren."

For some practicing Catholics, reconciling the teachings of the Catholic church and the teachings of the Bible could appear to present a dilemma. The phrase "being stuck between a rock and a hard place" comes to mind. Personally, I have always found that phrase to mean something quite different; personally, I find the choice easy. Let me explain. The key word in the phrase is "rock." If you believe that the Rock is Christ Himself, then the choice between a Rock and a hard place is really not so difficult a choice at all. Christ as the foundation "rock" is discussed in more detail in Chapter 3.

In summary, the news from Second Vatican Council was not very different from other councils for those outside the Catholic church. While most Catholics saw the immediate changes in the execution and the language of the sacrifice of the mass, still others found it far too proximate to "Protestant theology." A careful examination of the wording of the council discloses no softening from the acrimonious doctrines of earlier papal decrees and councils, and in particular the Council of Trent. Observers of both sides of the issues still await the good news from Second Vatican Council.

---

| Three things you should know after reading this chapter. |
| --- |

✝   Jesus loves you. Man changes his habits and traditions. Churches change; some dissipate; new ones spring forth. God is the same yesterday, today, tomorrow, and for eternity.  Since God is love, His love for us never ceases.

✝ Jesus seeks a relationship with you.  We should not postpone the consummation of this relationship.  Once we have accepted Him, we need to work at our relationship with the Lord as much as any other relationship.  Our relationship with Him is eternal.  We have the confidence of anticipating the enjoyment of His forthcoming kingdom.

✝ Jesus wants you to love your brothers.  Share your relationship with Him with everyone.  Specifically, take your friends and contacts to a Bible teaching church.  Reach out to your family members who may not possess the interest that you do in studying His Word.  Start a neighborhood Bible study.  Seek God's help and find a ministry that you can pour your heart into for His glory.

References

[1] Vatican II Principles taken from <u>Vatican II and the Extraordinary Synod:  An Overview</u>, Avery Dulles, Liturgical Pr., as reported in John XXIII Catholic Community Newsletter Vol. 6., No. 3, September, 1991

[2] Michael Davies, <u>Pope John's Council</u>, Arlington House Publishers

[3] CNS, "Mexican diocese formed as counter to Protestant influence," <u>People of God</u>, May 1992

[4] Ernest Falardeau, "Interchurch families celebrating baptism," <u>People of God</u>, February 1992

[5] Michael Parise, <u>Are We the One True Church?</u>, Liguori Publications, 1990

[6] CNS, "Lutheran-Catholic dialogue recognizes authentic Marian devotion is not idolatrous", <u>People of God</u>

[7] Jerrold M. Packard, <u>Peter's Kingdom: Inside the Papal City</u>, Charles Scribner's Sons

[8] Thomas Bokenkotter, <u>Essential Catholicism: Dynamics of Faith and Belief</u>, Doubleday & Company, Inc.

[9] Patricia Zapor, "Catholic immigrants find welcome at non-Catholic churches, <u>People of God</u>, August, 1992

[10] CNS, "Hawaii holy days dropped to Sunday plus two," <u>People of God</u>, May 1992

[11] Raymond E. Brown, "The Fundamentalist Challenge", <u>Catholic Update</u>, May 1990

[12] Fr. Art Perrault, "The Threat of Fundamentalism," <u>People of God</u>, April, 1990

[13] John Thavis, "Pope says constructive criticism useful," <u>People of God</u>, August, 1992

# Chapter 8

## The Best of the Rest

> *Salvation—*
>
> *don't leave earth without it!*

### Jesus Is Returning (and He Is Returning Soon)!

Evidence surrounds us and confirms the imminent Second Coming of Christ.  Read about the end times specifically in each of the synoptic Gospels:  in Matthew 24, in Mark 13, and in Luke 17 and 21.  Signs of the end times are also found in other places throughout Old and New Testament Scripture.  A small sampling of those signs follows.

The rise of a leader from the area of the former Roman empire is prophesied in Daniel 9:26.  The European Community (EC) (or one of its underlying treaties or pacts) may be that federation.  If it is not, the Bible promises the Antichrist will come out from what was the old Roman Empire.  The EC is assembling tremendous economic and military power and has stated an intent to foster a "peace for land" deal among Israel and its neighbors.  The EC may interfere with the land God has given the children of Israel.  The EC will require a "mark" on all goods that enter or leave their domain beginning in 1993; some have already cautioned this may be the forerunner of the mark of the beast.

The fall of Babylon is described in Revelation 18. Jeremiah describes a destruction upon Babylon so great no one will ever live in her lands again. Before Babylon can fall, Babylon must rise. Despite the premature claims of victory during the Gulf Crisis, Babylon (Iraq) continues to survive and amass its own arsenal of destruction. One year after the Persian Gulf War we learn that only about 25 percent of Iraq's SCUD missile launchers were destroyed. Some believers from the United States thought the Gulf War was the fulfillment of Jeremiah 50 and 51. Read through those chapters carefully and you will see Babylon will be laid desolate and never inhabited again. The "arrows of skilled warriors" are not the weapons in the Gulf war. The weapons in the Gulf War were effective but did not destroy as many targets as originally believed; weapons accidentally killed some of its own allies. Babylon's last chapter has not yet been witnessed–although it has been written.

Matthew, Mark, and Luke describe the earthquakes in various places. Earthquakes and storms continue to increase in number and intensity although man finds numerous explanations for them. One day after the earthquake that struck Los Angeles on June 28, 1992, the news carried the following assessment from some of its residents. They stated the likelihood of "the big one" grew more remote with every passing day; confident that the assortment of smaller quakes would offset the truly devastating quake. Fear shook portions of the state of California as after shocks continued weeks after the initial set of quakes. Somebody forgot to tell them the Bible says in Luke there will be "great earthquakes." The quakes we feel today are just a prelude for the forthcoming.

Daniel 12:4 forewarns us of the increase of knowledge in the last days. Certainly when we use knowledge to decrease our dependency on God and to increase our reliance on self, then knowledge becomes an idol. When man confabulates about the origins of the universe, the evolution of man, and the natural phenomena that explain the miracles of the Bible, we place ourselves above God's own Word and therein we falter and fail. God gave us an intelligence level unknown to the rest of the animal kingdom (for which some animals are probably quite grateful); yet, we are to use power of thinking to understand God; not to exalt ourselves to be like gods.

Luke 17:26 - 29 explains that in the days of the Son of Man it will be like in the days of Lot and Noah. Those Old Testament days were some of the most wicked that God tolerated (at least until He destroyed the evil with the fire and brimstone and the flood respectively.) Ironically, I am reminded as I write these words, that this week is celebrated by some as gay pride week. The 1992 Democratic platform was released and included abortion rights and gay rights towards the top of its agenda. The Supreme Court upheld a ruling that prevents prayer at high school graduation ceremonies while allowing the burning of crosses and the American flag as expressions of protected free speech. I believe Billy Graham is attributed with the quotation "if God doesn't judge the United States, he'll have to apologize to Sodom and Gomorrah." Murder, perversion, and the occult practices characterize our country moreso today than at anytime in its past.

Ezekiel 38 and 39 details the event of the people who will come in the last days against Israel from its far north. These are the people of Gog and Magog, the former Soviet Union, the old and new Russia. So many of these invaders will die while attacking Israel that it will take seven months to bury the dead. While many observers heralded the break-up of the old Soviet Union, the struggles of their various peoples have become evident. The control of their nuclear arms is unclear; thousands have been declared missing or unaccounted; others are suspected of being sold to nations unfriendly towards the nation of Israel–God's firstborn.

Revelation 9:16 numbers the mounted troops who cross the Euphrates; and that number was 200 million. While a sizable army, it is the size of which China has had for several years. Birth control policies in China today, allowing one child per couple, are causing millions of female fetuses to be destroyed until a male is conceived to carry forward the family name. Because of these policies, before the turn of the century, China will have tens of millions of war-age men with no women to marry. And so they too will have reason to descend upon other lands.

Matthew, Mark, and John's first epistle warn us about the false prophets; many who will portray themselves as the Christ. Jack Van Impe reported early in 1992 that there are over 500 self-proclaimed prophets in the state of California alone! The rising numbers of cults and memberships therein also testify to the "spirit of the antichrists that even now are already in the world" as John warned. New religions and old religions provide man with multiple lives through reincarnation, the promise that man will someday evolve into god through his own good works, and an opportunity to "tune into your cosmic consciousness." Under the Antichrist there will be a "world religion" before Christ's return but Satan will be at the controls, while Christ provides man with one last chance to turn towards Him. Persecution is promised to all those who do not bow down to the beast and worship him.

In Matthew 24:14 Jesus reminds us that the gospel of His Kingdom will be preached to the whole world and that then the end will come. Three times while composing this book I was reminded by separate ministries how the Gospel of Jesus Christ was being ministered via satellite throughout the world. Each ministry had a key role in getting the Word into the hearts of God's children and more importantly, those still needing a personal relationship with Him. Prior to the advent of satellite technology, worldwide accessibility to the Bible, was much more difficult. I believe that God enables man to use technology like satellites for the glory of God. In addition, a multitude of ministries are taking advantage of the open doors in the former Soviet Union to reach millions for Christ. Fortunately, the same "wall" that has kept Christianity away has also kept the cults away.

Despite the moral decay evident throughout the United States, there seems to be little indication that any hope exists for putting our prosperity back into God's hands. Instead, as a nation, we will receive judgment from God's hands. The economy, depleted by excessive imports and stressed by unending spending and debt, seems to be sustaining itself on fumes and false hope. The US will continue to decline in economic and military power and perhaps an expedited rapture or judgment is as much as we can look forward to as a nation.

Perhaps our attention and focus would be better directed if we looked at the end times in relation to the nation of Israel and the events taking place there daily.

First, there's Israel as the fig tree, the newly sprouted leaves, and its miraculous rebirth in 1948 after almost two thousand years of being scattered across the earth. We are quickly approaching the celebration of Israel's fiftieth anniversary as a reborn nation. Second, there are the preparations underway in Israel for Christ's return: plans to rebuild the temple (which must be rebuilt for the abomination of desolation in Daniel 9 and 11, and Matthew 24), the making of the temple garments and articles for temple sacrifice, the 1989 discovery of the anointing oil, the recent speculation about the return of the Ark of the Covenant, the search for the ashes of the Red Heifer, and the training of temple priests from the appointed tribes of Israel.  Third, is the desperation that people throughout the world seek for prosperity and unity.  Henry Spaak [1], an early organizer of the European Community epitomizes this desperation (emphasis mine).

> "What we want is a man of significant stature to hold the allegiance of the people and to lift us out of our economic morass into which we are sinking.  Send us such a man and, *be it god or devil, we will receive him.*"

Yes, the time is ripe for the appearance and the acceptance of the Antichrist.

The Lord promised to return His people into their own land, to be their Shepherd, and to keep His covenant with Israel.  The numbers of the children of Israel in the promised land have increased over 100 times in approximately the last 100 years.

Remember the Lord has kept His promises under what have appeared to man to be the most difficult of circumstances.

Many predictions have been made concerning the year 2000.  Many of those predictions have to do with the end of the world as we know it.  Many of those predictions about the world come from Christian leaders.  Finally, many of those predictions, concerning the year 2000 and the end of the world and by Christian leaders were offered by early church leaders almost two thousand years ago.

Both Christian and Jewish ancient documents contain evidences for a six thousand year existence of the earth.  The theory is supported by the quotation from Second Peter: "With the Lord a day is like a thousand years, and a thousand years are like a day."  Other Bible enthusiasts reflect on Psalm 90:4 with similar wording.  Some sources put the beginning of Old Testament time at about 4000 BC.  Since the Lord finished all His work in six days (Genesis 2:2) and rested on the seventh, a logical argument can be made that after six thousand years the Lord will bring in His millennial kingdom much like a "day of rest."  To complement this belief, is the prediction of early church writers that we would live two thousand years under the patriarchs, two thousands under the law, and two thousand under Grace.  My abbreviated summary of this theory is absent of many details that further substantiate its likelihood.

We are told to be ready and watchful. Only the Father knows the time that the Son returns. Nonetheless we have all been advised as to the events that would occur directly preceding His return (Matthew 24, Mark 13, and Luke 21). Those signs are increasingly apparent and surround us even now. We are reminded of those who were rewarded for waiting for Christ's first appearance.

> "Now there was a man in Jerusalem called Simeon, who was righteous and devout. He was waiting for the consolation of Israel, and the Holy Spirit was upon him. It had been revealed to him by the Holy Spirit that he would not die before he had seen the Lord's Christ. Moved by the Spirit, he went into the temple courts. When the parents brought in the child Jesus to do for him what the custom of the Law required, Simeon took him in his arms and praised God, saying: 'Sovereign Lord, as you have promised, you now dismiss your servant in peace. For my eyes have seen your salvation, ...'." (Luke 2:25 - 30)

Note Simeon's faithfulness, Joseph and Mary's obedience, and the keeping of the Spirit's promise. I do not pretend that the Spirit has given me any message of seeing the Second Coming. Nor do I pretend that I am righteous and devout. But I do know that He is my salvation.

Simeon was not the only awaiting Jesus' birth. Luke continues

> There was also a prophetess, Anna, the daughter of Phanuel, of the tribe of Asher. She was very old; she had lived with her husband seven years after her marriage, and then was a widow until she was eighty-four. She never left the temple but worshipped night and day, fasting and praying. Coming up to them at that very moment, she gave thanks to God and spoke about the child to all who were looking forward to the redemption of Jerusalem." (Luke 2:36 - 38)

The numbers presented in these verses indicate that Anna had spent a number of years in the temple. And she did, as we should, give thanks to God. And she did, as we should, speak about the child. And she did, as we should, anticipate the redemption of Jerusalem. Paul reminded Timothy:

> "Now there is in store for me the crown of righteousness, which the Lord, the righteous Judge, will award to me on that day—and not only to me, but also to all who have longed for his appearing." (2 Timothy 4:8)

Paul reminds Timothy that He will reward all who long for His appearance. My motive in longing for His return is to see Him and to live under His dominion and love; for we shall be able to thank and praise Him for all eternity.

A number of detailed books on prophecy identify these and other arguments for the proximate return of Jesus Christ. Today, Grant Jeffrey and Jack Van Impe (and Ezekiel, and Daniel, and Isaiah, and Jeremiah, and Paul, and John) are some of my very favorites. The Lord gave us prophecy so that we would know the signs (not the time) of His return. He reminded us to always remain vigilant and prepared.

## Selling Life Insurance vs. Sharing Life Assurance

One of the things I will always remember about growing up was how hard my dad worked; both day and night, weekday and weekend, in sickness (I don't remember him ever being sick) and in health. Most of my years at home he worked full-time during the day and sold life insurance at night and on weekends. I remember, even then, the decision not to spend as much time away from my family as he did. He just seemed to work all the time. Unfortunately I think that I have been less than dutiful in fulfilling that desire over the past few months and not spending the time I would prefer with my own family.

My preference would be to spend time with them and others sharing life assurance, assurance that comes from and through Christ Jesus. In part that's why I included three points to consider at the conclusion of each chapter. We need to realize His great love for us; His desire to spend time with us; and His desire that we share Him. While I don't agree with the notion, a number of folks discount the value of life insurance after the death of the insured. Of course, their perspective is based solely on the value of the policy to the insured at time of payment. When we have life assurance the assured retains great value after death; and even more advantageous, the assured shares in the other benefits of knowing Christ even before "cashing in" the assurance.

As examples, we enjoy knowing that He intercedes for us (Hebrew 7:25); that He is the only God and sole mediator for us (1 Timothy 2:5); that His name is the only name by which we can be saved (Acts 4:12); that in both the present and the age to come, there is no higher name in authority (Ephesians 1:21); and that while He reminds us not to sin, He defends us before the Father when we do (1 John 2:1). We have from now until eternity, the greatest intercessor, the greatest mediator, the only name to call upon, the ruler of all ages, and the greatest defender. No wonder David proclaimed "The Lord is my shepherd." He didn't say that He will be my Shepherd or might be my Shepherd but rather that He is my Shepherd. No wonder Moses called Him provider; Isaiah called Him the cornerstone; Matthew saw Him as the majestic king, and John saw Him as the King of Kings and the Lord of Lords.

## What's It To You?

The sometimes intimidating question "What's it to you?" when posed in a life threatening situation, is actually quite appropriate before Christ. We are all dealing with a life threatening situation. We are all dealing with the life after this earthly visit. Who's told you the story of Christ's salvation and His atonement for all of us? How did you respond? How did the message of the Bible measure against the traditions of your family and church life? Do you love Jesus enough today to put your life in His hands? We know He loves us enough to accept each and every one of us who comes to Him.

My life started again on my nineteenth birthday. I was in the service, stationed in Hawaii and had attended Bob Hope's USO tour earlier that day having shook hands with Miss America, Vida Blue, and other prominent members in the show. In a set of unrelated circumstances, later that same night, a young man about my own age introduced me to God's prominence. He led me in a prayer of salvation. His name was Tom. I have not seen him since leaving "the islands." I did not associate with him much thereafter but he made a difference in my life for which I am thankful.

Exactly nineteen years later, another Tom was preparing to baptize me in accordance with Scripture. I was now a believer trying to live by and grow in faith. I wanted to acknowledge His saving Grace before man. I desired to step forward in obedience to Him; to repent and be baptized. Because of special Christmas events at our church I was unable to be baptized on my 38th birthday. I opted to wait for the following week instead of being baptized at another location where I thought my own witness would be diminished. December 23, 1990, was the coldest December day ever recorded in New Mexico; yet I was warm.

This Tom, too, I thank for having listened to me. During a Christmas party in 1989, while acquaintances were discussing their New Year's resolution, I stated that for my family, I wanted the 1990s to be the decade of the Christian family. Tom heard that message. He invited me to a Bible study which I was asked to lead two years later. My wife and I were experiencing frustration in the teachings of the three Catholic churches we had tried over eight years. Tom invited me to the Sunday school class he attended, but I thought I would be struck dead at the mere entrance to a non-Catholic church. What a difference a Bible teaching church can make in the life of a believer in Christ!

Even as I reflect on the years in my life, I see Christ was with me every step. This young man's name was Bill. As a college student, he worked two summers at a church I frequented to play basketball. He coordinated summer leagues for the high school kids in the area. He marked and painted the first lines with us on the basketball court that most people thought was a parking lot. I remember he was a college football player and I believe a receiver. He was very strong in appearance but very quiet in spirit. He was a role model we should have shown more interest in emulating.

Ron was another Christian who shared with me. Ron worked at the gym on Carswell Air Force Base in 1971; another strong and powerful guy. I believe it was on a Saturday morning he invited me to go with him to meet with some other Christians for some prayer and fellowship. At eighteen I had no idea what fellowship was. I remember asking Ron where the donuts came from (I wanted to pay my share). He responded that God provided the donuts and it probably took a few years before I had any real idea of what he meant. Ron, thanks for your sharing.

I mentioned Mary much earlier in the book. She was there during a time of great turmoil in my life. I was arrogant, confident, and nothing like what I want to be today. But Christ was trying to reach me then while I was growing rich in worldly wisdom and self-reliance. Still He did not let me drift too far.

When I met my wife, she had one Christian lady friend in particular who had been witnessing to her. Joyce has been the most Godly woman I have ever known; for her love just never stops flowing. Thanks to Joyce, my wife was able to have a high regard for God's Word; work that I should have been doing and work that I need to do far more of even today. Thanks to Joyce, my wife and I know God works in the believers' life today.

Thank you, Lord, for each person you have sent into my life and thank You for the ones You will send into my life. For some testify they believe Your Word and so they do what you have commanded, yet for me I know you have already done things I cannot do and because You have completed what I cannot, what remains for me is to believe. When Jesus spoke of the difficulty the rich man would have entering into the kingdom of God "like a camel through the eye of a needle" He reminded us that with God all things are possible. The changes He has made in my life are evidence of the changes He can bring forth. Yet for me there is another message in Christ's metaphor: That the rich man leans too often on his own understanding and confidence obtained through worldly amassed riches and knowledge. Proverbs presents this principle

> "Trust in the Lord with all your heart and lean not on your own
> understanding; in all your ways acknowledge him, and he will
> make your paths straight." (Proverbs 3:5 - 6)

When we turn to Him I think we need an NIV; that's a new IV (intravenous). We need different feeding, a nourishment that only comes from dwelling in His Word; sustaining teaching that comes from the Scriptures. In order to "walk the talk" we need to "know the talk." Before we can act right by Him, we need to know right by Him. John tells us why the right teaching is necessary

> "Anyone who runs ahead and does not continue in the teaching
> of Christ does not have God; whoever continues in the
> teaching has both the Father and the Son." (2 John 9 - 11)

Very early in the first chapter I referenced the spiritual war in which we are all involved. My war is against the enemy of God. For the enemy has disguised himself so that he might deceive us and lead us off the straight and narrow path to Christ. Don't fight naked—put on the whole spiritual armor of God found in Ephesians.

"Stand firm then, with the belt of truth buckled around your waist, with the breastplate of righteousness in place, and with your feet fitted with the readiness that comes from the gospel of peace. In addition to all this, take up the shield of faith, with which you can extinguish all the flaming arrows of the evil one. Take the helmet of salvation and the sword of the Spirit, which is the word of God. And pray in the Spirit on all occasions with all kinds of prayers and requests. With this in mind, be alert and always keep on praying for all the saints." (Ephesians 6:14 - 18)

Keep your armor on forever. Be prepared to be attacked knowing He has already provided the victory when we know Him.

## Who Do You Say That I Am?

I would like to return to the two questions posed to Peter in Matthew 16. Who do others say that I am? Secondly, who do you say that I am?

Jesus answers His own question in the translation to the phrase "I am." This is the same phrase He used in response to Moses when Moses asked whom he should tell the people spoke to him. We can see our God throughout every book of the Bible.

| In the Book of ... | He is the ... |
|---|---|
| Genesis | creator of the universe and the cleanser in the flood |
| Exodus | great I AM and the provider in the desert |
| Leviticus | giver of the law |
| Numbers | administrator of manna |
| Deuteronomy | prescribing legislator |
| Joshua | leader of our household |
| Judges | conqueror with Gideon |
| Ruth | model of unselfishness |
| Samuel | answerer of Hannah's prayers |
| Kings | faithful one to the obedient |

| Chronicles | life in the dedicated temple |
|------------|------------------------------|
| Ezra | rebuilder of Jerusalem and His temple |
| Nehemiah | renewer of the dedication |
| Esther | rescuer of His people |
| Job | righteous restorer |
| Psalm | constant subject of our praises |
| Proverbs | provider of wisdom |
| Ecclesiastes | driver of the wind that is chased |
| Song of Songs | passion of our praises |
| Isaiah | responder before we call and the Immanuel |
| Jeremiah | keeper of the 70-year promise |
| Lamentations | sorrow of His people |
| Ezekiel | tribulation upon Jerusalem |
| Daniel | protector in the lion's den |
| Hosea | faithful bride groom |
| Joel | judge at the valley of Jehoshaphat |
| Amos | life and death of Israel |
| Obadiah | deliverer on Mount Zion |
| Jonah | demander of obedience |
| Micah | promised Babe to Bethlehem |
| Nahum | judge of Nineveh |
| Habakkuk | faithful rebutter |
| Zephaniah | forecaster of fire |
| Haggai | giver of careful thought |
| Zechariah | might in our spirit |
| Malachi | rewarder of the tithe |

| Matthew | author of the beatitudes |
|---|---|
| Mark | detester of tradition |
| Luke | leaper in the womb |
| John | Way to the Father |
| Acts | Holy Spirit poured out among us |
| Romans | worker of all things towards good |
| Corinthians | giver of gifts |
| Galatians | truth that sets us free |
| Ephesians | answerer of immeasurably more than we ask |
| Philippians | one who completes the good work He began |
| Colossians | nailer of the law to the cross |
| Thessalonians | catcher in the clouds |
| Timothy | truthful teacher |
| Titus | grace of salvation that appears to all men |
| Philemon | intercessor for the faithful |
| Hebrews | definer of faith |
| James | granter of good and perfect gifts from above |
| Peter | Living Stone in Zion |
| John | defender before the Father |
| Jude | warning to the godless |
| Revelation | triumphant redeemer crowned in glory |

He is who He says He is. He is the God of Abraham, Issac, Jacob, you and me. He is the God of Israel. He is the guest of highest honor at the marriage supper of the lamb. He is all powerful, all knowing, and always present. That's who I say He is.

Who do others say He is?  He's been called a prophet of God by some.
He's been called a "godly" man by others.  He's been called a lunatic
and a liar.  He's been called a revolutionary, a cosmic spirit and an
intergalactic traveler.

What are some of the Scriptural accounts of who others said He was?
In Matthew 3:17 the Father called Him His Son.  In Matthew 8:6 the
centurion called Him Lord.  In Matthew 19:16 the rich young man called
Him teacher.  In Mark 10:51 the blind man called Him Rabbi.

Even His enemies, the allies of Satan knew Him.

> "Just then a man in their synagogue who was possessed by an
> evil spirit cried out, 'What do you want with us, Jesus of
> Nazareth?  Have you come to destroy us?  I know who you
> are—the Holy One of God'!"  (Mark 1:23)

In Mark the demons knew Him and obeyed Him for they knew He was
greater than they.

> "For Jesus had said to him, 'Come out of this man, you evil
> spirit!'
>
> Then Jesus asked him, 'What is your name?'
>
> 'My name is Legion,' he replied, 'for we are many.'  And he
> begged Jesus again and again not to send them out of the area.
>
> A large herd of pigs was feeding on the nearby hillside.  The
> demons begged Jesus, 'Send us among the pigs; allow us to go
> into them.'  He gave them permission, and the evil spirits
> came out and went into the pigs.  The herd, about two
> thousand in number, rushed down the steep bank into the lake
> and were drowned."  (Mark 5:8 - 13)

Again Jesus tamed the spirit in Luke and all who witnessed were
enamored with His greatness.

> "Even while the boy was coming, the demon threw him to the
> ground in a convulsion.  But Jesus rebuked the evil spirit,
> healed the boy and gave him back to his father.  And they
> were all amazed at the greatness of God."  (Luke 9:42)

Thus far we have seen whom I believe He is, whom those who saw Him
believed that He was, and who even the demons knew He was (some
through verbal acknowledgment, others implicitly through their

obedience to Him). Who did Jesus say that He was? Was He crazy or possessed? Who would validate His claim or serve as a witness to His identity? I will present just three (of many potential) brief responses found in the book of John. First, He revealed Himself to the woman at the well.

> "The woman said, 'I know that Messiah" (called Christ) "is coming. When he comes, he will explain everything to us.'
>
> Then Jesus declared, 'I who speak to you am he'." (John 4:25 - 26)

Second, Jesus attempts to convince the Jews what He was not demon-possessed. Listen to His message and their response:

> "'I am not possessed by a demon,' said Jesus, 'but I honor my Father and you dishonor me. I am not seeking glory for myself; but there is one who seeks it, and he is the judge. I tell you the truth, if anyone keeps my word, he will never see death.'
>
> At this the Jews exclaimed, 'Now we know that you are demon-possessed. ...'" (John 8:49 - 52)

Third, Jesus is the supreme witness to His own identity in John:

> "In your own law it is written that the testimony of two men is valid. I am one who testifies for myself; my other witness is the Father, who sent me." (John 8:17)

If anyone is unconvinced by the evidence available through the Bible or believes His deity is unconfirmed by the evidence available today, we will all have the chance to see Him when He returns at the hour only the Father, His witness, knows. And when He returns and judges the nations and their inhabitants, we need to be prepared to know that we know and accept who He said He was. We need to know Him as our personal savior first and foremost. Know Him personally and directly while His invitation remains. The time has never been shorter and our need never more urgent. Be prepared to answer that same question He once posed to Peter–"Who do you say that I am?"

## The Last Exodus

Most of us are familiar with the story of Moses and how he delivered the people, as God's servant, from the hands of Pharaoh. As one of the most famous stories in the Bible, the Exodus showed God's faithfulness to His people. He showed He had not forgotten them. He showed that He could provide the rescue under the most difficult circumstances. He showed us that He rescues us from our tribulations and that He does not intend that we avoid every persecution; actually, we are promised quite the opposite for following Him.

Moses did not want to play a key role in the Exodus and many of us today do not want to play the key roles that God has determined for us. Like Moses' efforts, God's plan seems a bit too risky to man. As the tribes of Israel professed so many times, they would be content to be the slaves of Egypt rather than the rulers of the land of milk and honey.

When the Israelites returned from Babylon after their seventy year exile, very few actually returned to Jerusalem. History records that about 90 percent of those allowed to return actually stayed in Babylon. Those who stayed adopted the traditions of the peoples of that area.

Some Bible scholars have theorized about the "second Exodus" as the children of Israel are returned to their promised land in the final days. Some have speculated that just as the Egyptians pursued the fleeing slaves, to their own deaths, so too might modern day "Egyptians" change their hearts and pursue God's firstborn in the last days. This idea is certainly plausible and time will tell what God already knows.

I am personally waiting for the "last Exodus"; the one initiated by the trumpet call. This "Exodus" is described in Thessalonians.

> "According to the Lord's own word, we tell you that we who are still alive, who are left till the coming of the Lord, will certainly not precede those who have fallen asleep. For the Lord himself will come down from heaven, with a loud command, with the voice of the archangel and the trumpet call of God, and the dead in Christ will rise first. After that, we who are still alive and are left will be caught up together with them in the clouds to meet the Lord in the air. And so we will be with the Lord forever. Therefore encourage each other with these words." (1 Thessalonians 4:15 - 18)

From these verses we know who will be in this "Exodus"—those who are still alive at His coming. We know what will signal its start—a loud command from the archangel and the trumpet call of God. We know we who are still alive will not be first. We know where we are going—into the clouds. We know whom we will meet there—the Lord Himself. We know how long we will be with Him—forever.  We also know why Paul gives us this insight—to encourage each other.

This event is also known as the rapture.  It seems very similar to the Exodus from Egypt.  God hears the cries of His people.  God gathers His people.  God leads them supernaturally to a better place.  God promises to dwell with them forever.  Therefore, be encouraged.  Be encouraged in Christ.  Look forward to His second coming.

I suspect that more than anything else, I hope for and find comfort in is knowing that He is coming again.  His next coming is a source of ongoing joy; although, not too many of my friends would describe my joy as constantly or blatantly obvious.  In a way, I unintentionally give them the wrong impression.  I do not want you to receive the wrong impression.  Let me tell you that I have not played fair; that's right, I peeked ahead.  I've read the conclusion.  I've read how it all turns out in the end.  The final chapter was written approximately 1900 years ago and I read it before the other books.  And I've read it many times since.  And all the other books also.  It's all in there.  It's for you to see.  It's intended that you should know.  It's God's gift to man.  It's God's gift to you.  It's His Word.  Read again for the first time.

## Could You Be Convicted of Being a Christian?

One of the overused words I have become personally sensitive to in the early 1990s is "challenged."  Everything is just a challenge today for somebody.  Of course there are the personal challenges and, worse yet, the challenges we put upon ourselves.  I have challenged myself concerning the evidence of my own Christianity.  If I were brought before a jury of peers, would a reasonable person find me "a Christian?"

If the evidence was seized in my house, car, place of work, my attitude, and my contacts, what would they say?  Am I impatient in traffic?  How do I respond when cutoff or when there is someone moving noticeably slow in front of me?  I must admit that the evidence may not be there.  Despite the praise tapes that may be keeping me company or the Christian talk show to which I may be listening or the programmed radio settings for Christian stations, sometimes my heart does not feel and I do not act as God would prefer me.

What about my time at home?  I still act wrong with my wife.  I still holler at my kids.  I still get annoyed at appliances that fail.  I might spend my time in front of the television watching primarily Christian programming. I might have my VCR programmed to tape John Ankerberg. I might have my radios set to Christian stations. My VCR and audio cassettes may be heavily slanted towards my favorite Biblical teachers. I might conduct Bible studies with my family. I might supply them with Christian alternatives in literature. I might keep alcohol, drugs, and pornography out of my home. Yet I still do not imitate Christ (Philippians 2:5) all day long.

What about in the workplace? If someone was to sit at my desk would they be encouraged in Christ? As much as I love my job, I am still disappointed with decisions at time. I am still frustrated by those who openly and disparagingly describe God. I am disappointed most when I disappoint others, whether that be in teaching or helping them solve common problems (and quickly). I do not witness as much as I could at work. Yet I do seek fellowship and prayer with a few strong Christians at work. I do keep the Scriptures in my desk. I do keep Scripture on my desk and old Christmas cards reminding me of Christ's birth and promises on my desk. I do encourage other Christians at work for maintaining a Christian presence in their immediate work space.

What about the clothes I wear. In June of 1992 I took my family to Six Flags in Arlington, Texas. I made a point that day to notice the clothes that people were wearing that had a printed message. Actually I saw a number of shirts espousing Christ. Still, the majority of printed shirts carried messages about a sports hero or sports team, an alcoholic beverage, a death metal band, or a souvenir shirt from a bar. The shirts reflect the values of the people that wear them, consciously or unconsciously; intentionally or unintentionally. Do the clothes we wear model Christ or share His principles with those in whom we come into contact? Do we really do everything for the glory of God as one of the shirts subscribed?

What about the people I deal with in daily activities? Am I too often in a hurry when third or fourth (or second) at the checkout line? How do I treat a merchant when returning a defective item that has required considerable time for me to diagnose the defect? How do I treat my neighbors, their children, and property? How do I interact with a secular school system that outlaws Christmas, prayer, and disrupts family values?

When I consider the evidence for and against me, I am not so confident of the outcome. It's quite possible that the jury would find me "innocent" of being a Christian; that is, acquitted, unworthy. That's a frightening thought. The sentencing follows and Christ appears on the scene. He proclaims that the jury is right; without Him I am unworthy. And then He delivers the good news–through Him all things are possible. Through Him my sins have been paid in full. Through Him I am a child of God. Because He says, I am the Living Word. I am called Faithful and True. I am who I am. I am the King of Kings and the Lord of Lords. You have placed your faith in Me–enter My Father's Kingdom.

| Three things you should know after reading this chapter. |

✟   Jesus loves you. He tells us that the time is short. He offers us His atonement and the promise of His return. He desires that all of us know Him. He provided signs through the Scriptures to remind us that He had it all under control from the beginning. How has He shown His love for you?

✟   Jesus seeks a relationship with you. As we come to know Him and His Word, the signs that surround us all day, both of His graces and of His mercies, become that more obvious. The evidence of His love and our need for dependence on Him are reinforced with the apparent tribulations of the present world. Both directly and indirectly, what are the signs of His attempts to establish that relationship with you?

✟   Jesus wants you to love your brothers. Sharing His message of salvation, His warnings, and His signs require sacrifice of self and time; an abandonment of other things for God and His glory. The messages in this book are the best way that I know how to share with so many. Yet I desire that you read His book, not mine, which is why I have liberally placed the Word of true life on so many pages. Where else has God placed His Word in front of your heart so that you too might share its testimony?

References

[1] Jack Van Impe, "Watch History Happen," Perhaps Today, January/February 1993

*God's the authority -*

*not the majority!*

Trent, 47, 50, 64, 66, 67, 68, 85,
        89, 92, 128, 129, 135, 138,
        140, 141, 142, 145, 146, 149,
        150, 152, 155, 157, 162, 165,
        166, 167, 168, 174

**Vicar of Christ**, 72, 88, 164

**Word**, 18, 20, 22, 23, 25, 30, 31,
        35, 36, 41, 43, 44, 45, 47, 52,
        53, 55, 60, 62, 63, 71, 75, 76,
        77, 79, 82, 83, 85, 86, 87, 89,
        91, 92, 94, 104, 106, 107,
        111, 117, 120, 128, 132, 133,
        137, 139, 142, 145, 146, 157,
        160, 161, 163, 165, 171, 172,
        173, 175, 178, 180, 186, 193,
        195

**Zechariah**, 28, 30, 188
Zephaniah, 188

Favorite  Bible  verses  ...

**Things I need to remember ...**

Things I need to share ...

Special notes for family and friends ...

New personal commitments and dedications ...

**Escape from Purgatory has helped me in these ways ...**

# Mail Order Form

## 1. Complete the following send to information:

Company name:

_____

Name:

_____

Street Address:

_____

City:                    _____

State:                   _____

Zip Code:                _____-_____

## 2. Determine the cost of your product(s):

| Price | | |
|---|---|---|
| 1st book | 11.95 | |
| 2nd through 5th books | 9.60 | |
| **Sales Tax** (New Mexico shipping addresses only) | .69 (first book)  .56 (books 2 - 5) | |
| **Shipping** | | |
| 1st book | $2.00 | |
| 2nd through 5th books | $1.25 ea. | |
| **Total** | | $          . |

## 3. Send your check with this order form (or a copy of this form) to

Matthew 10:32 Ministries, ltd. co.
P. O. Box 20547
Albuquerque, N. M., 87154

## 4. Thank you!